ANDREW R. WHEELER

TOGETHER

IN PRAYER

Coming to God in Community

IVP Connect

An imprint of InterVarsity Press
Downers Grove, Illinois

5°CA

InterVarsity Press
P.O. Box 1400, Downers Grove, IL 60515-1426
World Wide Web: www.ivpress.com
E-mail: email@ivpress.com

InterVarsity Press® is the book-publishing division of InterVarsity Christian Fellowship/USA®,
a movement of students and faculty active on campus at hundreds of universities, colleges and
schools of nursing in the United States of America, and a member movement of the International
Fellowship of Evangelical Students. For information about local and regional activities, write
Public Relations Dept., InterVarsity Christian Fellowship/USA, 6400 Schroeder Rd., P.O. Box
7895, Madison, WI 53707-7895, or visit the IVCF website at <www.intervarsity.org>.

All Scripture quotations, unless otherwise indicated, are taken from the Holy Bible, New
International Version®. NIV®. Copyright ©1973, 1978, 1984 by International Bible Society.
Used by permission of Zondervan Publishing House. All rights reserved.

Design: Cindy Kiple

Images: Frank Krahmer/Getty Images

ISBN 978-0-8308-2114-3

Printed in the United States of America ∞

 InterVarsity Press is committed to protecting the environment and to the
responsible use of natural resources. As a member of Green Press Initiative we use
recycled paper whenever possible. To learn more about the Green Press Initiative,
visit <www.greenpressinitiative.org>.

Library of Congress Cataloging-in-Publication Data

Wheeler, Andrew R., 1963-
   Together in prayer: coming to God in community / Andrew R. Wheeler.
       p. cm.
   Includes bibliographical references.
   ISBN 978-0-8308-2114-3 (pbk.: alk. paper)
   1. Prayer groups. 2. Prayer—Christianity. I. Title.
   BV287.w48 2009
   248.3'2—dc22

                                                                    2009000465

P   22   21   20   19   18   17   16   15   14   13   12   11   10   9   8   7   6   5   4   3   2   1
Y   27   26   25   24   23   22   21   20   19   18   17   16   15   14   13   12   11   10   09

To Mom:
I wish you were here
to share this part of the journey with me.
One day we will share it in the presence
of him for whom this book is written.

CONTENTS

FOREWORD

THERE IS AN INCREDIBLE CONNECTION that happens through prayer between believers and the heavenly Father. It is something that intersects the physical with the spiritual and goes far beyond human comprehension. The ability for mankind to speak in the throne room of the Almighty is awesome in and of itself. But the fact that he, in all of his splendor, will stop and listen intently to our every word, as if nothing could be more important to him at that moment, is truly breathtaking. God desires relationship with us, and our dialog with him through prayer is where he reveals the deep things of his nature. Paul reminds us in the book of Philippians that our determined purpose is to become more deeply and intimately acquainted with God. There is great power in this fellowship, and *Together in Prayer* is your handbook through the journey.

Andrew R. Wheeler has obviously spent a great deal of time compiling this exploration of prayer, as it unravels some of the complexities of the multidimensional conversation, perhaps as never before. *Together in Prayer* is full of wisdom and insight into personal, community and intercessory prayer. You will be enlightened and challenged.

Honestly, as the senior director of the National Day of Prayer Task Force, I was thrilled to find such an outstanding book. We believe that community transformation begins where two or more are gathered together in God's name. In corporate, or community, prayer we can petition the Father in humility with great expectation that God will heal our land.

If you have been challenged to lead a small group in prayer or serve as a prayer coordinator, this book is a must read. You will be equipped and prepared to confront the mountains in our culture today. I highly recommend this resource and encourage you to read it cover to cover, again and again.

John Bornschein
Senior Director
National Day of Prayer Task Force

ACKNOWLEDGMENTS

THIS BOOK IS THE CULMINATION (to this point) of two journeys—a journey in community prayer, and a journey in writing. Only God could have molded these two journeys into one.

I owe the beginning of my journey in community prayer to Valley Christian Fellowship, the InterVarsity chapter at Saginaw Valley State University (then Saginaw Valley State College) in Saginaw, Michigan. Through late-night prayer meetings, one-on-one prayer times, conferences and other events, God introduced me to people who loved to pray together—people like Ken and Missy Binder, Tom and Barb Bishop, and several others. The times we spent in prayer together still rank as the pinnacle of my group prayer experience. Recapturing the fervor and fellowship we shared has been a lifelong ambition for me.

The next step in the journey was joining the International Ministries prayer team at Willow Creek Community Church. Sweet times of prayer and learning with Deanna Battreall, Tim Lennox, Jennifer Taylor and others both nourished and encouraged me. It was at this point that I began what turned out to be an early venture into writing about prayer, working with David Bulger to produce the IM prayer letter each month.

When the McHenry County regional campus of Willow Creek Community Church was formed, a handful of us met in the beginning to strategize and dream about the prayer ministry. Our "prayer, planning and quiche club" consisted of Susan Minatrea, Karen Franzen, Karen Graham and myself. I learned to think strategically about the prayer ministry with these wonderful colaborers, even as my manhood was constantly challenged by the "quiche" aspect of our team! These dear coworkers were also among my biggest supporters over the course of writing this book.

To date, this journey has led to my present area of service as codirector of the prayer ministry at Willow Creek McHenry County, a position I joyfully share with Jerry Lee. A better ministry partner one could not hope to find. Our core prayer team makes serving in prayer a privilege rather than an obligation.

The writing part of this journey actually started shortly after WCMC opened its doors. Our prayer team had planned for a time of training small group leaders to lead their groups effectively in prayer. I taught this session, and afterward several members of our team said that I should go further with it. I had never considered writing a book before, but I began to put down some thoughts that eventually became the book you now hold.

Any first-time author would tell you what I didn't know at the time—writing is by far the easiest part of the journey. Getting a book published is much, much harder. I had no idea how to even get started with that until a friend at Willow Creek suggested that I attend the annual Write to Publish Conference in Wheaton, Illinois, directed by Lin Johnson. June 2005 found me in great fear and trepidation hoping to meet with David Zimmerman (editor at InterVarsity Press) at this conference. The conference itself was literally life-changing for me; I've been back every year since. And that initial meeting with David led to another encounter at the 2007 conference and eventually to the publication of this book. David's interest in and encouragement for this project are largely responsible for this finished product.

No worthwhile journey is undertaken alone, and my journey is no exception. Besides the people I've already mentioned, I owe a debt of gratitude to Denny Brogan, our Inter-Varsity staffworker at Saginaw Valley; Denny is the one who first showed me what real vision and passion for ministry mean. Not many people are fortunate enough to have a significant lifelong friend, but I have such a friend in Mike Pollard, who has both encouraged me and led me spiritually; Mike published my first article in *ACMC Mobilizer.* Sue Kline, then editor of *Discipleship Journal,* patiently taught me much about writing for an audience in the course of publishing an article I wrote (and rewrote, under her tutelage!) called "How to Wake Up Your Prayer Times" (*Discipleship Journal,* November/December 2007). The many instructors I've had at the various Write to Publish conferences have gone a long way toward erasing my many deficiencies as a writer.

Anyone who is married knows that significant ministry is far more joyful, more rewarding and more fulfilling when it's shared with your spouse. My wife, Debra, has been my biggest encouragement all along. From putting up with my overcommitments to ministry, to reading and giving feedback on this book, to praying with me time and again during the ups and downs of writing and trying to get the book published, Debra has unswervingly supported and encouraged me. I'm grateful to have her as a life partner.

INTRODUCTION

"FEED MY HUNGRY CHILDREN." But there are so many!

"Make disciples of all nations." I don't even know where they are!

"Care for the orphan and the widow. Visit those who are sick and in prison." How do I get started?

"Love your neighbor as yourself." You mean, not just "don't hate my neighbor," but take actual steps to show love?

Over time, God has placed many different visions on my heart. Too many, in fact, for one person to make any significant difference in all of them. At times, I've been led to despair for all that I *couldn't* do in answer to the promptings of the Holy Spirit. In response, God has led me to one consistent answer: prayer. I can't reach all the unreached peoples, but I can get informed and pray for them. I can't feed all the hungry children, but I can care enough to pray for them (and I can feed a few!).

Even so, the needs for prayer seem nearly limitless, and

I'm still just one person. Like many others, I struggle to pray consistently for all the people and situations I know God is leading me to pray for. But the good news is, I don't have to. I'm part of a body, with people and groups to whom God gives different lasting passions.

What if all those groups could pray more effectively together, both for their own needs and for the needs of the world around them? That's the passion behind this book. I'm convinced that God's call to prayer is a call not just to individuals but to churches and groups as communities. Consider the following commands to pray in the New Testament:

> I urge . . . that requests, prayers, intercession and thanksgiving be made . . . for kings and all those in authority. (1 Tim 2:1-2)

> Pray for us, too, that God may open a door for our message. (Col 4:3)

> Remember those in prison as if you were their fellow prisoners, and those who are mistreated as if you yourselves were suffering. (Heb 13:3)

In the highly individualistic Western world, we personalize and individualize these commands, but originally these and other commands to prayer in the New Testament were given almost exclusively to *groups* of people. Just as being part of the body of Christ is a major component of what it means to be a Christian, so praying in community is a major part of what it means to pray.

Yet, praying in community is something that many Christians find very difficult, if they even try it at all. Many of us have been in group prayer times that seemed to drag on interminably, struggling to merely stay awake (let alone contribute). We've been part of group prayer experiences that left us feeling preached to rather than lifted up into God's presence. We've seen our group prayer times devolve into sharing and counseling sessions. And we've concluded that group prayer is at best a necessary evil. Even those among us who have strong personal prayer lives often leave times of group prayer feeling disconnected and uninspired.

It doesn't have to be this way. The church of our earliest records was united, regularly experiencing God's miracles and leaning heavily on God in prayer. Together, the believers sought God's wisdom in making decisions (Acts 1:23-26), his intervention in difficulty (Acts 12:5), his blessing on ministry (Acts 13:3), his strength in trouble (Acts 20:36). Group prayer times can be dynamic, exciting, fulfilling experiences that draw group members closer to God and closer to each other. They can be times of sweet, impassioned prayer for those in the group and times of passionate mission as the group focuses prayer beyond its own walls. Such prayer times can build unity in a group as almost nothing else can. Most of us don't regularly experience group prayer like this. This is not an intrinsic limitation of group prayer; rather, it's an outcome of the fact that, as a whole, we don't know how to pray together effectively.

This book is an attempt to help group members pray more effectively in a group setting and to help group leaders set the stage for community prayer times that will be a highlight of a group's life together. It's born of a fervor to see people pray together consistently, passionately and effectively; and of the conviction that concerted community prayer is the first step to solving many of the world's great problems.

Prayer in a small group setting is often referred to as "group" or "corporate" prayer, but I prefer the term "community prayer," as it is a closer reflection of the nature of effective prayer in a small group setting. In this book we will take a look first at some of the principles of community prayer. Then we'll discuss specific ways to keep community prayer engaging and vibrant. After exploring ideas for casting a vision for community prayer, setting the tone and leading the time, we'll conclude by applying community prayer concepts to other prayer settings, such as corporate prayer and one-on-one intercession.

The principles and ideas for community prayer apply to any type of small group. Whether you are a small group leader or member, and whether your group is a church small group, a campus group or a neighborhood group: if your group is struggling to establish a vibrant group prayer life, this book is for you. My prayer is that God will use the ideas and suggestions in this book to transform your group's prayer life into one of the highlights of your life together.

THE CASE FOR
COMMUNITY PRAYER

The closest that many believers come to group prayer is listening to a pastor pray from up front during the worship service. Prayer in the church today seems to be most often relegated to a few key leaders and perhaps a small set of people whose focus is to pray for the church.

Although we don't know for certain exactly how the New Testament church prayed together, it seems reasonable to believe that their experience of prayer was much more participatory than this. Phrases like "they all joined together constantly in prayer" (Acts 1:14), "they devoted themselves to the apostles' teaching . . . and to prayer" (Acts 2:42), "they raised their voices together in prayer" (Acts 4:24) and many others seem to portray prayer not as a spectator sport but as a participatory practice.

In many cases, the best way to move a church toward this participatory model of prayer is through the small group ministry. This is true for several reasons:

1. People are more comfortable praying with people they know than praying with strangers.

2. Small groups provide the best setting for a person to be fully known, and thus most effectively prayed for.

3. Small groups are usually a good place for encouraging spiritual disciplines, particularly community disciplines.

In spite of this, somewhat rare is the small group that consistently prays together effectively. In most small groups, prayer is limited to perhaps an opening prayer before the Bible study and maybe a closing prayer, plus perhaps a prayer for a crisis situation in one member's life. Consistent, ongoing prayer for life-change is simply not a part of the experience of most small groups; and yet, such prayer may be the single most empowering thing that a small group could do to develop Christlike character in its members.

Why is it that so few small groups pray together consistently and effectively? I can think of a couple of reasons. First, we fail to understand the importance of *community prayer*. We have personalized most of the examples and teachings of the New Testament to the point that we neglect their relevance to a community setting. Second, we don't know how to pray well together. Too often, small group prayer leaves group members flat and uninterested.

In the next chapter we'll consider whether there's a "right" way, according to the New Testament, to pray together. But first let's look at the importance of community prayer in the early church.

THE IMPORTANCE OF PRAYING TOGETHER

From Jesus' teaching to the practice of the early church to the commands and urgings of the Epistles, the New Testament paints the picture of group prayer as a normal part of the lives of believers and churches. Even before there was a church, Jesus clearly expected believers to pray together. The famous promise, "For where two or three come together in my name, there am I with them" is given in a context of praying together: "If two of you on earth agree about anything you ask for, it will be done for you by my Father in heaven" (Mt 18:19-20). This expectation also seems to be implied in the wording of the Lord's Prayer in Matthew 6.

> Our Father in heaven,
> hallowed be your name,
> your kingdom come,
> your will be done
>> on earth as it is in heaven.
>
> Give us today our daily bread.
> Forgive us our debts,
>> as we also have forgiven our debtors.
>
> And lead us not into temptation,
> but deliver us from the evil one.

Note that all the first-person pronouns in this prayer are plural, implying that it is meant primarily as a prayer to be prayed in a community setting.

In Jesus' time of greatest trial, in the garden of Gethsemane, he took with him the three most trusted disciples, asking them to keep watch with him and pray. Knowing the temptations they would face in the next few days and already

19

having predicted their denial of him, Jesus warned them: "Watch and pray so that you will not fall into temptation" (Mt 26:41). Jesus gave them each other to keep them watchful at prayer. How much more, two thousand years removed, does the church today need to be a body that prays together and keeps each other watchful?

Scripture doesn't provide much detail about how the early church prayed together, but we do know that it was the practice of the church to gather often, and a key component of that gathering was prayer. We read in Acts 1:14 that the disciples "joined together constantly in prayer." Acts 2:42 implies a commitment to praying in community, as the other key practices mentioned are all community practices.

We get a glimpse of an early church prayer meeting in Acts 4:23-31. The believers raise their voices together in praise to God after the release of Peter and John by the Sanhedrin. Again in Acts 12:12 we see the believers gathered together in prayer, presumably for Peter's release from prison. Barnabas and Paul are commissioned for their first missionary trip in a context of community fasting and prayer in Acts 13. Paul and his companions, when in a town too small for a synagogue, go down to a place by the river to pray together (Acts 16:13, 16). Paul and Silas hold a two-man "prayer meeting" in prison in Acts 16:25. Again, we find Paul praying with the Ephesian elders in Acts 20:36.

The church was begun in a context of prayer; the apostles and the earliest believers were in the habit of praying together regularly, and as the church grew and spread beyond Jerusalem, the focus on corporate prayer spread with it. In towns like Antioch and Ephesus corporate prayer seemed to be the norm. Again, we don't know exactly what that prayer looked like, but we do know that it was a focus of the earliest church and then of the missionary church.

The "rugged individualism" that so marks modern Western civilization has caused us to look at much of the instruction and narrative in Acts and the Epistles exclusively in terms of the individual. While there is no doubt personal application in these texts for the individual, Gene Getz, in his book *Praying for One Another,* points out that we miss the crux of these teachings when we ignore their corporate context. Consider the following commands regarding prayer from Paul's epistles:

- "Be joyful in hope, patient in affliction, faithful in prayer" (Rom 12:12).
- "Speak to one another with psalms, hymns and spiritual songs. Sing and make music in your heart to the Lord, always giving thanks to God the Father for everything, in the name of our Lord Jesus Christ" (Eph 5:19-20).
- "And pray in the Spirit on all occasions with all kinds of prayers and requests. With this in mind, be alert and always keep on praying for all the saints" (Eph 6:18).
- "Do not be anxious about anything, but in everything, by prayer and petition, with thanksgiving, present your requests to God. And the peace of God, which transcends all understanding, will guard your hearts and your minds in Christ Jesus" (Phil 4:6-7).
- "Devote yourselves to prayer, being watchful and thankful" (Col 4:2).
- "Be joyful always; pray continually; give thanks in all cir-

cumstances, for this is God's will for you in Christ Jesus" (1 Thess 5:16-18).

Certainly these commands all apply to individual believers, but they also apply to churches as bodies, especially since that's the audience for which they were originally written. These commands become richer when we realize that they are not just God's will for individuals but also God's will for his church. In addition, they become easier to observe when we can draw strength from one another as we obey them.

When Paul writes to the churches to "pray for us" (Eph 6:19-20; Col 4:3; 1 Thess 5:25; 2 Thess 3:1) and when the writer to the Hebrews asks the same thing (Heb 13:18), the context indicates that they should lift up these missionaries in prayer together, not just in their own private prayers. When we recall that these letters were written to be read aloud during church meeting times, it's not too hard to imagine the various congregations going straight to prayer for the authors of the letters as soon as they were read.

James, in possibly one of the most challenging exhortations to community prayer, urged the believers to "confess your sins to each other and pray for each other so that you may be healed" (Jas 5:16). Obviously, the only way to confess sins to other believers is to do so in a context of community. To James, confession, repentance and prayer were to be corporate acts, not merely individual ones.

Peter may have had something similar in mind when he spoke of the church being a "holy priesthood" (1 Pet 2:4-10). When he urges the believers to "be clear minded and self-controlled so that you can pray" (1 Pet 4:7), the context of loving one another and using spiritual gifts to serve one another clearly implies that he has in mind praying together. Perhaps he recalls in this verse Jesus' admonition to his inner circle of disciples in the garden of Gethsemane to "watch and pray."

PRAYER IN THE CHURCH TODAY

We can safely conclude that praying together was a significant part of the early church's life. What was it about community prayer that kept the early church praying together like this? Was it God's faithfulness in answering, even to the point of performing miracles? Was it the sweetness of coming into God's presence together? Was it the encouragement of being lifted up in prayer by those who knew them best? Was it maybe a combination of all these and more?

What was true of the early church is true of the church today: God reveals his power and his love consistently as the church seeks him in prayer. We can expect his blessing and direction in our lives as we come into his presence in prayer as a community. Community prayer, so important in the life of the early church, should occupy a similar place in the church today.

Unfortunately, the fact that community prayer is so important to the life of the body doesn't mean that it's also easy to practice effectively. Many groups that do actually pray together regularly struggle to pray well together. They keep plugging away because they know it's important to pray together, but their times of prayer are not as meaningful or effective as they could be.

Is it possible that the reason we don't pray well together is that we don't know how to pray together? Might there be some principles that could guide our times of prayer together and improve our community prayer lives? In the next chapter, we'll examine these questions in more depth.

QUESTIONS FOR REFLECTION/DISCUSSION

1. How do you picture prayer taking place in the early church?

2. What has been your experience of prayer in a group setting? Has that experience been positive or negative for you overall? How so?

3. Why might community prayer be less common today than it was in the early church? What are some of the hurdles to community prayer today?

THE DISTINCTIVENESS OF

COMMUNITY PRAYER

IF PRAYING IN COMMUNITY WAS so important to the New Testament church, why is it that the Western church today largely fails to practice community prayer? Even churches that strive to base themselves on the New Testament model often neglect this crucial area of life together. To help us understand this, let's consider the distinctiveness of community prayer and then some of the perceived difficulties in community prayer. We will then outline some principles for praying in community that can help us overcome these difficulties.

Prayer has many definitions in the church today, from the narrow sense of intercession to the broad extreme that our entire lives are a prayer to God. A middle ground would include different aspects of prayer, such as intercession, praise, confession and thanksgiving, but limit itself to conscious, deliberate acts of prayer. For the sake of this book I define prayer as "conversation with God."

Prayer styles differ from the highly liturgical on one hand through a more conversational model to, at the other extreme, praying in unknown tongues. Additionally, there are many different types of prayer. In his classic book *Prayer,* Richard Foster lists and describes several different kinds of prayer, grouped into three major categories: inward prayers (focused on the transformation of our hearts), upward prayers (focused on intimacy with God) and outward prayers (focused on ministry).

While some of these types and styles of prayer are best practiced privately, many of them find their fullest expression in community. God invites us into his presence in private settings, but he also invites us to come before him in community. Jesus' model prayer in Matthew 6 seems to imply a community setting. Have you ever felt that the burden of prayer was too much for you to carry, that there were too many things to pray for and not enough time? Community prayer strengthens and encourages us for the task by reminding us that we are part of a body, and the burden does not fall on any one individual. Thus, community prayer is distinct from private prayer in that it incorporates the body, functioning as one.

Community prayer is also distinct from community worship times in two major aspects: purpose and participation. Weekly worship gatherings generally serve several purposes. If you look at these purposes in terms of time spent on each, the primary purpose that emerges is instruction; secondary purposes include praise, imparting of information and fellowship. Community prayer has a more focused purpose: although there may be many topics, the focus of community prayer time remains on entering God's presence.

In terms of participation, weekly church gatherings for many take on a "spectator" dynamic. Personal participation is limited to singing a handful of songs and the obligatory "turn and greet." In more liturgical traditions, congregants may recite prayers, responsive readings or learned responses together. In neither case is there any significant unscripted engagement on the part of the average person.

Community prayer is more participatory, encouraging the contributions of each group member on a relatively equal footing. Group members participate as God leads them, within the established framework of the group meeting. No one individual or group of individuals dominates the time.

Our first difficulty with praying in community, then, stems from the fact that corporate worship doesn't train us in the kind of participation community prayer requires. Small groups provide more of a participatory environment, but many Christians are not involved in small groups, and most small groups do not focus on prayer as a primary purpose for their time together. Further, in many churches, prayer is seen as the specialty of a small group of people (a "prayer ministry") rather than something that should involve the entire body. Meanwhile, Scripture is often read in terms of the individual rather than in terms of community, a consequence of the individualism of the West. Most Western Christians thus don't expect community prayer to be part of their walk with God; most of our prayer experience remains private.

Beyond that, community prayer requires a certain amount of vulnerability within a group—a willingness to occasionally stumble for words or not know how to address a particular topic. This level of vulnerability generally comes only with time spent together. In his book *Making Room for Life,* Randy Frazee develops the thought that we live in multiple worlds that rarely intersect. We work with different people than we worship with, and we live among a third group different from either of those two. Children's activities can bring us into another entirely distinct world. A few communities, such as the Amish, seem to have retained the idea of living in one coherent world, but for most of us in the West, this is a constant struggle. Besides leading to an overly frenetic pace of life, being spread out among all these diverse worlds means that we don't get to know people in any of our worlds as well as the early church knew each other. As a result, the vulnerability needed for effective community prayer is largely absent in the church today.

The early church's more community-based lifestyle forestalled much of the discomfort we have today with community prayer. They naturally practiced the spiritual disciplines, including prayer, in a context of community. The time spent together in various basic activities increased their vulnerability to each other, making it easier to pray together. And the fact that they lived in one coherent "world" provided both the time needed to pray together and the environment in which this occurred naturally.

Given the lack of practice of community prayer in today's church, it isn't surprising that this type of prayer often scares people off. Uncertain expectations in terms of participation, accountability and vulnerability contribute to a fear of the unknown. Performance pressure (real or imagined) makes us wonder if our prayers will "measure up" to those of others in the group. The variety of prayer styles makes us uncomfortable. Perhaps negative experiences with group prayer in the past linger in our minds and make us reluctant to venture out again.

Not only do we lack experience in praying together, we also lack instruction. Foster notes in *Celebration of Discipline* that Scripture doesn't instruct us specifically in many of the spiritual disciplines because the early church did not need instruction on how to practice them; early Christians were already familiar with them. Given the differences between the early church and the church today, and given the lack of specific instruction in the Bible on praying together, how much of the early church's prayer experience can we reasonably expect to re-create?

This may be the wrong question to ask. The goal should not necessarily be to re-create a two-thousand-year-old environment but rather to take some of the principles that guided the early church and apply them to our environment. While the Bible does not give us specifics on how to run a prayer group per se, there are several biblical principles that can help us to pray more effectively in a group setting. For the remainder of this chapter, I'd like to take a look at three of those principles: humility and simplicity, orderliness, and love.

HUMILITY AND SIMPLICITY: THE RIGHT WAY TO PRAY

Probably Jesus' best-known teaching about prayer is recorded in the Sermon on the Mount. In this sermon he gave the disciples a format to follow that has become known as the Lord's Prayer. As an introduction to that prayer model, he gave these instructions:

And when you pray, do not be like the hypocrites, for they love to pray standing in the synagogues and on the street corners to be seen by men. I tell you the truth, they have received their reward in full. But when you pray, go into your room, close the door and pray to your Father, who is unseen. Then your Father, who sees what is done in secret, will reward you. And when you pray, do not keep on babbling like pagans, for they think they will be heard because of their many words. Do not be like them, for your Father knows what you need before you ask him. (Mt 6:5-8)

What was wrong with the way the "hypocrites" prayed? Their prayer flowed from hearts full of pride. They pretended to be expressing thanks to God but were really bragging about themselves in the presence of others; they sought not God's blessing, but others' admiration. Elsewhere, Jesus condemns the teachers of the law for making lengthy prayers for show but having in their hearts no mercy or kindness (Mk 12:40; Lk 20:47). Again, the pray-ers sought honor from men, not blessing from God. Such honor will be all that results from their prayers: "They have received their reward in full" (Mt 6:5).

Jesus' next words are not meant to forbid praying in a group setting but rather to show a contrast: secrecy versus publicity; prayer to an unseen Father versus prayer to be observed by others; "reward" in the eyes of others versus response from the sovereign God.

Jesus similarly contrasted prideful prayer with the kind of humble prayer that God hears in Luke 18:9-14, the parable of the Pharisee and the tax collector. The Pharisee "stood up and prayed about himself" (Lk 18:11), while the tax collector desperately and humbly pleaded for God's forgiveness. The Pharisee's reward? Everyone who heard his prayer knew how much he thought of himself. The tax collector's reward? Forgiveness from a gracious God.

One of the great temptations in community prayer is praying for others to hear, and not for God to hear. We will examine this more thoroughly in a later chapter, but for now suffice it to say that the same principle of humility before God that is so important in private prayer is also critical to community prayer. Nothing is more damaging to a time of community prayer than a person praying long, flowery prayers designed to impress or excite others in the group.

Jesus was also an advocate of simple, brief prayer: "Do not keep on babbling like pagans, for they think they will be heard because of their many words" (Mt 6:7). The admonition is reminiscent of Elijah's great contest with the prophets of Baal, who prayed long and loud to their unhearing god— with no result. When Elijah's turn came, he prayed a very simple prayer to the One God who sees and hears: "O LORD, God of Abraham, Isaac and Israel, let it be known today that you are God in Israel" (1 Kings 18:36). The God who sees and hears doesn't need many words to figure out what the petitioner is asking for; indeed, he knows our needs even before we ask (Mt 6:8). So a simple prayer, focused on God's kingdom and God's will, is best.

Humility and simplicity in prayer are closely related, as Jesus' words demonstrate. Pride is the source of long, flowery prayers designed to impress others. Humility expresses itself in simple, heartfelt entreaties to a gracious, loving God. Jesus modeled such prayer in Gethsemane (Mt 26:36-44;

Mk 14:32-39; Lk 22:39-44). He prayed desperately, earnestly and specifically, but briefly and with total submission to God's will. Again on the cross, Jesus uttered very simple, very heartfelt prayers to God. He didn't need to impress the onlookers with long, high-sounding prayers; he simply needed to connect with his Father.

Such is also our need in community prayer. In community prayer we invite God's supernatural presence into the lives and situations of group members. Our need is not to pour out a litany of information to God, as though he did not already know it; nor is it to gain the approval of group members for how "well" we pray. Rather, our real need is to simply connect with God and fix our thoughts and our hearts on him.

Orderliness: The Right Way to Worship

The church at Corinth, in terms of its worship times together, was a mess. Their worship services were lengthy, but not life-changing encounters with God for the congregation. The problem? Everyone was participating as he or she saw fit, without regard to others who wanted to participate and without regard to how their participation would or would not build up the body. People were speaking in tongues without intepretation, prophesying "as the Spirit moved them" and generally acting as if no others were present. To correct this, Paul gave instructions in 1 Corinthians 14 about orderly worship. Although his instructions are not specifically about community prayer, their general applicability to corporate gatherings makes them very relevant to our topic.

It is interesting to note that Paul's instructions here have nothing to do with the condition of the believers' hearts. It could be that the believers were worshiping in such disorganized ways because of pride in their own gifts, but Paul gives no indication of this. He does not speak to sin but rather to the logistics of the worship service itself. This is not intensely "spiritual" instruction for the believers, but it is necessary if they are to worship God in a way that will honor him and will draw the body near to him.

What we find in this passage is that there is more to effective corporate worship than simply the condition of the believers' hearts. To be sure, hearts must be humble before God for worship to be effective. But there must also be a sense of orderliness; otherwise, the "worship" degenerates into a chaotic, "everyone does as he sees fit" experience that benefits neither God nor the participants. The same may be said of community prayer.

Our community prayer times are much different from a first-century worship service, so we're not going to delve deeply into the specific rules that Paul gave. Rather, we will focus on the principles on which those rules are based. What principles from Paul's teaching can we gather and apply to community prayer?

First, we find the principle of wide participation in the worship service (1 Cor 14:26). Paul recognizes that everyone wants to participate and that everyone has something to contribute (how wonderful if our prayer meetings were this way!). He affirms the appropriateness of this participation ("all of these must be done"). Our times of community prayer should likewise be times in which all can participate. Not all will participate in exactly the same way, but the time is not to be dominated by one person or a few people.

Second, Paul speaks to the idea of orderly worship by giving instructions on how to have such widespread participation in an orderly way (1 Cor 14:27-30). The worship service is not to be chaotic, with everyone participating as they see fit whenever they see fit. "God is not a God of disorder but of peace" (1 Cor 14:33). This principle of orderliness is given not to restrict the worship of the community but to guide it in such a way that all can participate in the service. Rather than a steady stream of people speaking in tongues, one at a time is to speak, and only if there is an interpreter. In this way, the entire congregation benefits from what is spoken. Again with prophesying, limitations are placed in order to permit the congregation to digest what is said and so to benefit from it. Picture a gathering with numerous people speaking in tongues and others prophesying, and the words flowing so quickly that the congregation at large can't keep up. This is what Paul is trying to correct.

The idea of orderliness in worship has its application to community prayer. For the group to truly be of one mind and heart as they pray together, the members need to be able to understand and enter into the petitions of the person praying aloud. Picture a prayer meeting with no orderliness, no agreement, no oneness of heart and mind. Or picture a prayer meeting where everyone prays what is on his or her mind with complete disregard for what has already been prayed. Again, there is no agreement, no unity.

Paul elsewhere remonstrates with the Corinthians regarding the way they observe the Lord's Supper. They each partake as they see fit, without waiting for one another (1 Cor

11:21). They ruin much of the intent of the observance by failing to participate as a community. Their observance is simply a bunch of individuals each acting for themselves, rather than a community observance of the Lord's Supper. In fact, Paul goes so far as to say that it's not really the Lord's Supper they are eating, their practices being so far removed from what Christ taught and modeled (1 Cor 11:20). Participating as a true community requires waiting for each other and partaking together.

Likewise, community prayer should be a time of participating as a fellowship, as a community. This is not just a gathering of individuals each doing as he or she sees fit, but rather a concerted time of seeking the Lord together. Paul's instructions for orderliness in worship and observance of the Lord's Supper clearly speak to our times of community prayer. Personal prayer styles and preferences need to be subject to the good of the group in community prayer.

Love: The Right Way to Relate

As prayer is an expression of a relationship with God, so community prayer is an expression of a community's relationship with God and with each other. Scripture abounds with teaching about how believers should relate to one another in community, and this teaching has relevance to community prayer as well. We will look at just a couple of examples here.

The disciples occasionally fell into the trap of self-exaltation. They argued about who was the greatest among them (Mk 9:33-34; Lk 9:46-48). They excluded others from using Jesus' name to drive out demons (Mk 9:38; Lk 9:49). They rejoiced that demons submitted to them in Jesus' name (Lk 10:17). James and John wanted to make a showy display of destroying a Samaritan village that did not welcome Jesus (Lk 9:54) and coveted the exalted positions at Jesus' right and left hand (Mk 10:35-37). Peter boldly and proudly declared that he would never deny Jesus even if the rest of his followers abandoned him (Mt 26:33; Mk 14:29; Lk 22:33).

Each time, Jesus rebuked and corrected their self-centeredness. Instead, he taught them to love one another (Jn 13:34). The self-exaltation that occasionally marked their behavior was the very antithesis of love and could have destroyed the community had it gone unchecked. Therefore, Jesus never left this attitude unchallenged. He modeled love and humility—the very things he was trying to teach the disciples—by washing the disciples' feet.

Paul also emphasized the priority of love. He contrasted it in 1 Corinthians 13 with some of the "spiritual" practices that people often exalted themselves with rather than God. He exhorted the believers to act out of love for one another (Col 3:12-14) and to honor each other above themselves (Phil 2:3-4). John's letters are full of commands to love one another; he even points out that love for one another is a reliable test of whether or not we really know God (1 Jn 4:7-21). In fact, this is the way Jesus said people would know who belonged to him (Jn 13:34-35).

The principle of relating to one another in love extends to our community prayer times. When we truly listen and join in with the prayers of others—rather than just focusing on our own requests—we are showing love to others in the group. When we pray for one another, we are showing love.

When we restrict our own tendencies in prayer in deference to others in the group, we are showing love.

PRAYING IN COMMUNITY

If there is a right way to approach God in personal prayer, and if there is a right way to relate to God in corporate worship, and if there is a right way to relate to other believers, then it is not much of a stretch to think that there might be a right way to pray together. Of course, this "right way" has a lot to do with the attitudes of the heart, as is the case in personal prayer, corporate worship and the fellowship of believers. But there are also some very practical, very specific results of those attitudes that can enhance and empower our times of community prayer. As we practice principles like humility, love and orderliness, we will find some general guidelines and some more specific applications to community prayer.

Many prayer groups fall short of experiencing all that God has for them in prayer because of a failure to recognize that there are principles to guide our community prayer times. Afraid of offending group members, leaders may shy away from laying down "rules" for the time of prayer. While we naturally accept (even demand) a certain orderliness and design in our corporate worship times, recognizing that there is meaning to the elements, the order and the content of the worship service, we somehow resist similar ideas when applied to community prayer.

If you've ever led a small group Bible study, then you know that certain principles, such as staying on topic, keeping the study focused on the passage at hand and interpreting in context, contribute to a more meaningful Bible study time. And while these principles restrict the "freedom" of members to contribute any ideas that may pop into their heads, the end result is a far more focused and helpful Bible study with a much better chance of accurate and meaningful application.

Community prayer is much like this. If we submit to one another and to the group and follow certain principles to guide our prayer times, then we will inevitably end up with a much more meaningful and God-honoring prayer time than if everyone participates as he or she sees fit. And while this may at first seem like a bit of a sacrifice of individuality in prayer, we must recognize that the Christian life is not primarily about individuality—it is about growing into Christlikeness in a context of community. Group prayer, practiced on principles like love, humility and orderliness, provides one of the best possible environments for such growth.

QUESTIONS FOR DISCUSSION/REFLECTION

1. Have you ever been in a prayer setting where everyone was praying as they saw fit? Describe the experience and your reaction.

2. Have you ever prayed with someone who was evidently proud of the way they prayed? How did their prayer affect you?

3. Read Ephesians 5:15-21. How might the command to "submit to one another out of reverence for Christ" apply to community prayer times? What do you think this would look like?

AN AUDIENCE OF ONE

COMMUNITY PRAYER IS TO PRIVATE PRAYER what a symphony is to a solo. An orchestra playing together—with various sections picking up refrains from each other, with chords dependent on the contributions of multiple instrumentalists, with a beautiful collective voice raised to the audience—this picture begins to describe the ideal of group prayer.

Often, however, group prayer turns out to be more like a collection of soloists each playing their own piece than a concerted voice arising out of teamwork. One particularly experienced soloist plays a very long piece, and others are intimidated to follow. Multiple soloists each play a piece of their own, but there is no relationship between the pieces, no common refrain. The result is a cacophony of individual prayers and not true community prayer—not the picture Jesus had in mind in Matthew 18:19-20 when he spoke of two or more people coming together and agreeing in prayer.

One of the main reasons we tend to struggle in community prayer is that we fail to recognize its two-dimensional nature. Private prayer concerns itself with only one dimension: the relationship between the believer and God. Community prayer, however, adds a second dimension: the relationships among the believers who are praying. Balancing these two dimensions of prayer is not always an easy task.

Community prayer at its best can be defined simply as "praying to God with people." The definition is simple to articulate but not always easy to follow. Even those who have strong personal prayer lives often struggle with balancing the vertical and horizontal relationships in community prayer. Accustomed to private prayer, they can sometimes forget that they are praying in concert with other believers and end up praying in ways that may not be appropriate in a group setting.

"Praying to God" means that we address God—not the group—in prayer. Our prayers are focused on asking God to intervene in situations and in people's lives, not on changes that people need to make. Praying to God means that we're praying always for his will, submitting our requests to him but not demanding that he answer in a particular way. We're trusting that he will answer according to his perfect wisdom (and acknowledging that our wisdom is imperfect). Finally, praying to God means that even as we pray over temporal circumstances, we're focused on "kingdom prayers"—prayers that emphasize God's eternal work in the lives of those for whom we're praying.

"Praying with people" means that as we pray, we keep in mind the presence of the community of believers. We pray in concert with others in the group, limiting our prayers so as to invite participation of the whole community, and agreeing with one another as we pray. We enter into the prayers of others in the group, rather than focusing strictly on our own concerns. We develop a true community conversation with God, rather than a series of one-on-one conversations.

While most of the prayer problems that Jesus addressed stemmed from heart issues, many of the most common problems in community prayer are caused not by sinful hearts but simply by a failure to understand some of the implications of the two-dimensional nature of community prayer. In this chapter we'll discuss the first dimension: community prayer as directed at God. In chapters to follow we'll explore the second dimension.

The Pharisee and the Tax Collector

By "praying to God" we mean that we are praying for God to hear, not for people to hear. The primary audience of our prayers is almighty God. When we bring our petitions to him, we trust him with the outcome. We address God directly in our praise, thanksgiving and petition, inviting his supernatural presence in the group and claiming his sovereignty over the situations that we bring to him. We take comfort from his presence and mercy, and we express gratitude for his intervention in our lives.

On the other hand, when we pray for people to hear, the audience of our prayers is the group with which we're praying, not God. "Prayers" addressed for the group to hear can be meant to teach, to exhort or to inform, or they can be meant simply to exalt the one praying.

One of the best biblical illustrations of the difference between praying to God and praying to people is in Luke 18:9-14: two men pray, one for people to hear and one for God to hear. The Pharisee in this parable was praying not for God to hear but for the tax collector. Had he been praying to God, there would have been no need to pass on the information about his fasting and tithing—God already knew that. But the true motivation of the Pharisee was to compare himself (favorably, of course) to the tax collector, and to let the tax collector know how righteous he was. Note the wording of the Pharisee's prayer: not "I thank you that *you* . . ." but rather "I thank you that *I* . . ." The Pharisee claims to thank God, but in reality he is merely expressing pride in himself.

The tax collector, on the other hand, prays a prayer of desperate earnestness for God's forgiveness. No pride is expressed here, and the audience is God alone—there is no attempt to impress anyone else with his prayer. Jesus concluded that "this man, rather than the other, went home justified before God."

Praying for the group to hear is not always the result of a prideful heart; it can be an unintentional result of recognizing the presence of others. One quick test that can be helpful in determining if our prayers are truly addressing God or addressing others in the group is to ask the question, "Would I pray this way if I were alone?" If the answer is "no," if the prayer would become meaningless prayed in the closet, then there's a good chance that the one praying is addressing the group, not God.

Another key to identifying who is being addressed in prayer is to listen to the subjective pronouns being used. If the subject of a sentence is *you* (for example, "Will you help me?"), then God is being addressed. But if the primary subject of a prayer is *I, we* or *he,* then the prayer is being aimed (sometimes unintentionally) at someone else. In the case of the Pharisee, the pronoun most common in his prayer was *I.* "I am not like . . . I fast . . . [I] give . . ." This was clearly a prayer that was all about the Pharisee.

Typically, prayers like this are not prayers to God but different ways of addressing the group. Most of the time, the motivation is not so obviously selfish. The result, however, is still that God is not honored and his sovereignty is not recognized or invited. Let's look at a few examples.

EXHORTATION

Consider this prayer: "Father, may we be more sensitive to those outside the kingdom and may each of us reach out to our lost neighbors." Prayer like this can come from the purest of motives— that of seeing the lost come to Christ—but it is not really so much prayer as it is exhortation of the group. Note the pronouns: "may *we* be sensitive . . . may *each of us* reach out." God is not addressed in this

> **T I P :** *Pay attention to the subjective pronouns you're using. If you use a lot of* I, he, we, they *pronouns, you are primarily addressing people, not God. If you use primarily* you, your *prayer is addressing God.*

prayer; nothing has been asked of him. Instead, the believers in the group have been asked to be more seeker-sensitive and more open to their neighbors. The group members may indeed need to do that, but the time of prayer is not the time to exhort them. Prayer is for addressing God.

Besides the fact that God is not addressed in a prayer like this, the effect on the group can be very disheartening. Those who are not actively reaching out to their neighbors are left feeling guilty about that and probably "preached to" (an accurate feeling). But because this exhortation is couched in terms of prayer, there is no opportunity to respond, no chance to discuss the problems that group members might have in evangelism. Those who are actively witnessing to their neighbors are left feeling unacknowledged, as though the one praying expects still more of them. The pressure is on each group member to "get with it" in evangelism, and the result is much more likely to be discouragement and defensiveness than motivation.

How could the above prayer be shifted in focus so that God is the one addressed, and his presence is invited into the lives of group members? "Father, would you please give us each more and more of a heart for the lost, and please bring into our lives people who need you. Open doors for us to share the gospel." In this prayer, God is the one being addressed. Nothing at all has been asked of the group members (other than implicitly that they would agree in asking God to do these things). Instead, God is asked to act: to give a heart for the lost, to bring people into our lives, to open doors and so on. God's sovereignty is thus acknowledged and his presence invited into the lives of the group. He is honored as the Source of a heart for the lost, rather than the group being exhorted to somehow develop this heart on their own.

We can all agree that we need God to act in our lives with respect to our hearts for the lost and to open doors for sharing the gospel. Here the group is not pressured into action; instead, God is invited to do a work in the group members. This sort of prayer both honors God and implicitly encourages the believers, leaving group members expecting God to act, whereas the first example leaves God out of the equation and puts pressure on the believers.

INSTRUCTION

A subtle (and closely related) way in which we often address people rather than God in prayer is by giving instruction. The Bible has many examples (e.g., Neh 9) of people reciting instances of God's faithfulness in prayer. Often such recitations are an encouragement to the people listening that, as God has been faithful in the past, so he will be again. There's a distinction here between *corporate* prayer and *community* prayer. Corporate prayer happens when one leader prays on behalf of a crowd of people, and it often takes on an element of instruction. In community prayer, a group of equals prays to God together.

Consider the following: "Lord Jesus, you tell us that it is to the Father's glory that we bear much fruit. But the only way we can do that is if we remain in you, the vine. Lord, we are branches in that vine, and we need to remain in you." There is nothing wrong with what's said here. Couched in terms of community prayer, however, it is out of place. Jesus did not need to be told that we need to remain in him; he already knew it (indeed, he said it first!). The crowd is instead being reminded that they need to remain in Jesus if they are to be fruitful (note the repetition of the pronoun *we*). This prayer asks nothing of God, but rather is offered as a reminder to the believers.

How might such a prayer look if it were addressed to God, rather than to the group? "Jesus, forgive us for the times when we attempt to bear fruit on our own and not in your strength. Remind us in those times that you are the vine and we are the branches. Draw us often to yourself; be the Source of our strength and fruitfulness." Many of the same words are used in this prayer as in the first one, yet all of the requests are being made of Jesus, not of the group members. The verbs are all directed toward him: *forgive, remind, draw, be the Source.* A prayer like this may indeed remind believers that they need to remain in the vine, but it does much more—it asks Jesus to get involved rather than just leaving it to the believers to figure out.

COUNSELING

People sometimes couch counseling in terms of prayer. Again, counseling has its place, but consider the following: "Lord, Joe really needs to feel your presence and to understand that you are guiding him each step of the way. He needs to trust this situation to you and have faith that you will do what is best."

> **TIP:** *If you're addressing God in prayer, then God should be the subject of most of the verbs in the prayer. The verbs should be things you're asking God to do.*

This prayer is all about Joe and what he needs to do in his situation. Joe is told to focus on God's presence, to trust in his guidance and to rely on his sovereignty. God is asked to . . . well, God isn't asked to do anything. After such a prayer, Joe probably feels gently chided for not having a stronger faith. He is reminded that he should realize that God is with him and that God has the situation in control. Joe may need to be reminded of that, but prayer is not the place to remind him.

"Father, please draw near to Joe and give him a sense of your presence. Grant him your peace and strengthen his faith to trust in you." This prayer, far from being all about Joe, is all about God and what the one praying is asking God to do in Joe's life: draw near, give, grant, strengthen. The verbs are all things that the group member is asking God, not Joe, to do. Rather than Joe being asked to have a stronger faith, God is asked to strengthen Joe's faith. Joe is left leaning on God. The distinction is somewhat subtle, but important— and the one being prayed for can definitely sense it.

INFORMATION

Another way we tend to address people rather than God in prayer is in the sharing of information. Instinctively we realize that others in the group may not know the circumstances surrounding a particular prayer, so as we pray, we provide those details. We end up praying for people to hear. Our motives are well intended, but still the focus is taken off of God.

> **TIP:** *Share information about prayer requests before the actual prayer time; this helps keep the focus of the prayer time on God.*

A group should enter the time of community prayer informed enough to pray for the people and circumstances that will be the topics of prayer. This means that whatever sharing needs to take place should happen beforehand. People should be free to ask questions for clarification and get the details they need in order to pray.

A word of caution: many groups get so caught up in the sharing of the requests and all the minute details surrounding them that the time of prayer is limited. Often, more time is spent talking about praying than actually praying. We need to remember in our sharing time that the goal is simply to provide enough information to enable group members to pray effectively.

Sermonizing

Occasionally, someone will use a time of community prayer as a platform for a "minisermon." Consider the following: "Father, may people who are far from you come to our church today. They need to hear your Word and realize their need for you, rather than pursuing their own selfish desires. They need to repent and receive Jesus as their Savior, to save them from a Christless eternity. Their lives need your touch; may they stop making excuses and come to meet you today."

Minisermons like this tend to focus on something that someone else needs to change. The focus of the prayer may be one or more persons in the group or it may be people outside the group, as in this example. The point is that in any case, the focus is not on God—nothing has been asked of God in this prayer. Further, although such a prayer can be motivated primarily by God-honoring intent (such as the desire to see the lost saved), there is often a bit of hidden pride in a prayer like this, based on an implied comparison between the people being prayed for and the one praying (*they* need to be saved because, unlike me, *they* are lost).

A prayer like this can be prayed in such a way as to focus on God rather than on people. For example: "Lord, please bring to our church today people who are far from you. Free them from anything that may be keeping them from knowing you. Break down any barriers that are in their way, and draw them by your grace." This type of prayer has the same primary motivation—the salvation of the lost—but focuses on God's activity in bringing the seeker to himself, rather than on the lostness of the seeker. Refocusing these prayers on God helps to remove any judgmentalism and the implicit pride that can accompany it.

CHEERLEADING

In some faith traditions, loud, almost shouting prayer is a normal practice. Determining whether such a prayer fits into the category of "cheerleading" has to do more with the content and aim of the prayer than with the manner in which it is prayed.

In his book *Piercing the Darkness*, Frank Peretti paints a picture of a prayer meeting at which a woman named Donna takes the floor and addresses a long litany of encouraging, "cheerleading" words to the gathered believers. Their focus is shifted away from God until the pastor eventually reins Donna in and redirects the group's praying toward God. Donna, we come to learn, is actually working against the church.

Not all cheerleading prayer has such subversive motives, of course, but the effect can often be the same. Rather than focusing on God, the group is led in prayer to a view of life in Christ that, though not directly unscriptural, ignores whole realities of who he is and what he does. The problem with cheerleading prayer is this lack of balance and the resultant limited view of God and his work in the life of the group. For community prayer to be effective, the vertical relationship of a group with God, more so than the horizontal relationships of each group member to the others, must be kept in view.

REMEMBER THE VERTICAL

When a pray-er prays for the group to hear rather than addressing God, the vertical dimension of community prayer is ignored.

Sometimes, such prayer stems from issues of the heart. Someone who thrives on acknowledgment from the group speaks spiritual truisms in prayer and receives the anticipated "amens." Someone who wants a platform to make an observation waxes eloquent about the situation in the world (or the church, or whatever). Someone who feels that there is a problem in the group uses the prayer time to share their sense of the problem. Someone who has just learned or experienced something exciting spiritually longs to share that with the group. The setting of prayer somehow seems to legitimize these impulses. Biblical instruction and interpretation (even misinterpretation) can be shared without correction; the group can be exhorted without being given a chance to respond. Such prayer not only fails to lift the group into God's presence but often can harm the unity in a group.

On the other hand, many times practices like these stem simply from a lack of understanding of the difference between praying *with* people and praying *to* them. As you approach a time of community prayer (particularly petition and intercession, which occupy most of our community prayer time), remember to focus on asking God to act. Pay attention to the pronouns you are using to make sure that you are indeed addressing God rather than others in the group. This may seem mechanical at first, but as you make a conscious effort to address God in prayer, you will find that prayer lifts you more into God's presence, strengthening your faith.

If you find that your tendency in prayer is to address the group rather than God, don't despair. This does not necessarily invalidate your prayers or call into question your motivations. Instead, it highlights an opportunity to not only move closer to God in prayer yourself but also help your group move closer to God.

One way in which I learned recently that I was focusing a bit too much on myself in prayer had to do with the way I asked God to do things. I never really noticed how many times the word *I* crept into my prayers until I heard my pastor pray a few times. He tends to word his requests, "Lord, would you . . ." By contrast, my typical prayer form—"I pray that you would . . ." is really a very unnatural way of stating a request. We'd never ask a friend to do us a favor by starting with "I ask that you would . . ." As I began to emulate my pastor's wording, I found that my mind focused more on God than on my act of making a request. The mechanics of prayer really can have a positive impact on the focus of the heart.

QUESTIONS FOR DISCUSSION/REFLECTION

1. Have you ever prayed with someone whose prayer seemed addressed to you? How did you feel?

2. What differences do you see between the following two prayers?

   "Lord, may people come into church today prepared to hear your Word."

   "Father, please prepare the hearts of the people who come to church today to meet with you."

3. What phrases do you commonly use in your prayers? To what degree do they "mechanize" your praying?

4

SEEKING GOD'S KINGDOM

IRONICALLY, THE VERY THINGS FOR WHICH we pray can
themselves be distractions to us. We focus our attention on
the people and circumstances for which we pray rather than
on the God to whom we pray. The distinction can be subtle,
but it is important. The Lord's Prayer (Mt 6:9-13) provides
not just a good outline for prayer but also a context in which
prayer—even prayer for personal needs—can retain a focus
on God and not be distracted by temporal things.

HALLOWED BE YOUR NAME

When Jesus started the prayer with "Our Father in heaven,
hallowed be your name," he wasn't just stating one in a line
of requests. He was providing the context in which the entire
prayer (and, by extension, our prayers) should be prayed.
Whether this phrase is seen as praise (your name is honored) or as petition (may your name be honored), the focus
on honoring God's name is not just a quick nod in God's di-

rection before getting to the real "meat" of the prayer. Rather, honoring God's name is the goal of the entire prayer, and should be the goal of our prayer lives as well.

Like private prayer, community prayer has honoring God's name as its primary goal. "Hallowed be your name" should be the common thread woven throughout all that we pray, whether in praise and thanksgiving, confession, intercession or petition. This context for prayer benefits our community prayer times in many ways: we're more inclined to focus on addressing God rather than people; we're more likely to pray in God's will, as opposed to emphasizing our own agendas; and (as we shall see later), we're more likely to be able to agree together in prayer.

Jesus' next phrase, "your kingdom come," is both a specific request and a context in which the remainder of the prayer is offered. Jesus was concerned with the forming of God's kingdom on earth in general and in the hearts of his disciples in particular. He wanted God's will to be done in the lives of those whom he taught, and on earth as a whole.

The coming of God's kingdom is not a separate idea from his will being done. It is as his will is done in our lives that his kingdom is established in us. If all that we pray and all that we ask God for is prayed in a context of God's kingdom and will, then we can know that we're on the right track in prayer. Focusing on God's kingdom and his will lifts our hearts and minds heavenward and can help us avoid the distractions often present in prayer.

"Your will be done" is not a prayer that encourages us to sit back, throw up our hands and say, "Whatever." Rather, it's a prayer that provides a context in which we ask God to provide for our specific needs.

The remainder of the Lord's Prayer—petitions for God's provision, forgiveness and guidance—can be seen in the context of these first three phrases. As temporal creatures, we cannot pray for or accomplish God's will outside a temporal context. If God's kingdom is to come in my life, it must come in a context of my physical body, my ability to earn a living and provide for my family, and hundreds of other temporal circumstances. This is the only context in which I live, and Jesus acknowledged that in the Lord's Prayer. It honors God to provide for our needs (daily bread), and it is his will to guide our lives. But such prayer should always be offered in the context of God's will and kingdom.

Seek First His Kingdom

A relatively small (but close) moon can obscure a much larger (but farther away) sun during a solar eclipse. Similarly, our relatively small needs can eclipse a much larger God when we focus our attention on them rather than on him.

Contrast this focus with Jesus' command in Matthew 6:33 to seek first God's kingdom. Although this command was not given in the immediate context of prayer, the larger context likely indicates that the "seeking" to which Jesus referred included prayer. Consider Jesus' specific requests in the prayer we've been discussing: "Give us today our daily bread. Forgive us our debts, as we also have forgiven our debtors. And lead us not into temptation, but deliver us from the evil one." Jesus could have gone into all the details about exactly why God's provision of daily bread was needed or just how great the need was, but instead he simply asked God to provide it. The prayer was specific but not overly detailed.

This is not to say that we should not bring our requests to God. Indeed, in the very next chapter, Jesus specifically commands us to ask God to provide for our needs (Mt 7:7-11). Focusing our prayer on the requests rather than our Provider, however, often leads to long, drawn-out prayers of the kind that Jesus warned against in Matthew 6:7. Similarly, focusing on the details of our needs tends to weaken rather than strengthen our faith. We see the obstacles and fail to appreciate fully in faith God's ability to overcome all obstacles. Picture the Israelites on the verge of crossing into the Promised Land, standing at the edge of the flooded Jordan River. Had they concerned themselves with the depth and speed of the water, the number of children who couldn't swim, the difficulty in getting all their possessions across the river, they may never have taken that first step of faith into the water. Instead, they focused on God and stepped out in faith. Focusing our prayer on God strengthens our faith and invites him to do a supernatural work.

When our prayers are focused on specific results that we want to see God bring, we may miss alternate ways in which God chooses to act. By specifying how God should answer a prayer, we risk weakening our faith when God chooses to answer in a different way. You've probably heard prayers like this many times: "Father, please grant Les a good interview tomorrow because he's been without a job for six months and he really needs to be able to support his family. His children have been sick and he needs the medical insurance, and the time out of work has put a strain on his marriage." This prayer takes the focus off God and puts it on Les's situation, providing information that God does not need. If Les is present, it probably discourages him to think about having been out of work for all that time and causes him to worry about providing for his family.

Shifting the focus to God and away from Les yields a prayer like the following: "Father, thank you for your provision for Les's family during his time of unemployment. Thank you for the interview that he has tomorrow. Please grant him favor in the eyes of the interviewer, and if this job is your place for him, please open that door." Les, if he's present, is going to appreciate this prayer much more than the first one. Why? First, he is reminded that God has indeed been faithful (but reminded in a way that honors God rather than preaches to Les). Second, the pressure is taken off him. Imagine how differently Les will approach tomorrow's interview having been prayed for in this way, as opposed to the first prayer! Note also that a prayer that is focused on God's activity (rather than on the circumstances) more naturally leads to thanksgiving, as God's past activity is recognized.

It's important to remember here that God already knows what we need before we ask him (Mt 6:8). He does not need a lot of information and he does not need to be updated on recent developments. While we should pray specifically and not just in vague generalities, we also need to remember that it is an all-knowing God who led us to pray in the first place, and he is the one who puts on our hearts what to pray for.

This is not to say that there is no place for pouring our hearts out to God, as so many of the psalms do. God understands our need to communicate verbally to him our deepest, most desperate desires; in fact, he made us to do just that. But unless the group is fairly close and intimate, the time of community prayer may not be the best place for this. Such prayer may find its best expression in the prayer closet.

PRAYING GOD'S WILL

For Jesus, praying for God's will to be done was not just something he taught; it was something he practiced. In his time of greatest trial in the garden of Gethsemane, Jesus asked quite naturally that some other way be found to accomplish God's purposes than his own torture and death. He subjected that prayer, though, to the Father's will: "Yet not as I will, but as you will" (Mt 26:39).

John gives us this promise regarding praying for God's will: "This is the confidence we have in approaching God: that if we ask anything according to his will, he hears us. And if we know that he hears us—whatever we ask—we know that we have what we asked of him" (1 Jn 5:14-15).

There are some things that we can pray for with complete confidence that we are praying God's heart in the situation. We can ask for the salvation of an unbelieving friend or family member; we can pray for revival in the church; we can ask for God's wisdom (Jas 1:5). These are prayers that God delights to answer. He will answer in accordance with his own character and plan, however; it won't do any good, for example, to ask that an unbelieving friend be saved even though he refuses to acknowledge Jesus Christ as his Savior. Prayer for salvation is necessarily prayer that a person would come to know Jesus Christ.

Other issues are not always as clear-cut, however. Does it

please God to have us ask for his financial provision or for healing from a particular illness or injury or for other temporal things? Or are these things too mundane to be subjects of prayer? Most Christ-followers know instinctively that God wants to provide both our eternal salvation and our temporal needs. Those instincts are correct; as we've seen, Jesus acknowledged as much when he told the disciples to pray, "Give us today our daily bread" (Mt 6:11). God already knows the things that we need in our earthly lives, so we are not to become preoccupied with these things in prayer (Mt 6:32-33). But Jesus encouraged us to ask God for these things (Mt 7:7-11), and consistent with this, Jesus practiced thanking God for earthly blessings like food (Mt 14:19; 15:36), recognizing God as the source of earthly blessings. James also reminds us that "every good and perfect gift is from above, coming down from the Father" (Jas 1:17).

The apostle Paul prayed that God would remove a specific difficulty (often taken to be a physical illness or weakness), and God specifically refused to do that (2 Cor 12:7-9). Indeed, God had a specific purpose for this difficulty—to keep Paul from becoming conceited. Paul was forced, in his weakness, to rely on God's strength—making Paul much stronger than he would have been otherwise (2 Cor 12:9-10). Was Paul wrong to ask God for relief? Scripture does not directly answer that question, but based on other passages regarding prayer, it seems reasonable to believe that Paul was not wrong to pray in this way. In fact, it could well be that the very act of praying about this situation opened Paul's heart to see God's greater purpose in his suffering.

Suppose Paul had never asked God for relief. Would he have ever heard the words, "My grace is sufficient for you, for my power is made perfect in weakness"? It seems reasonable to interpret that as Paul opened his heart to God in prayer, God in response showed him the higher purpose in his suffering. Paul accepted God's will as being the best plan, even though it didn't exactly correspond with his own hopes for the removal of the "thorn." God's plan wasn't the most convenient for Paul, but we can be sure that it was the plan that best advanced God's purposes through Paul. So Paul was right to pray for the desires of his heart and he was also wise to accept God's answer. Paul submitted his own desires to God's will, as Jesus did in Gethsemane.

God wants us to bring to him our temporal needs. He delights in providing for us, and he wants us to acknowledge that he is indeed the Source of every good gift. To fail to bring our needs before him is tantamount to saying that he is either incapable of or uninterested in providing for us, or that we are fully capable ourselves of providing for our own needs. As we bring our needs to him, we acknowledge him as Jehovah Jireh, our Provider. Trusting God to provide for our needs is one way of honoring his name.

At the same time, God wants us to be concerned first and foremost with his will being accomplished. He wants us to come to him trusting and believing but not demanding, to submit ourselves to him (Jas 4:7) and our requests to his will, as Jesus did. To refuse to pray in this context is to insist that we know better than God does. As we submit to his will, we acknowledge his wisdom, his goodness and his grace in our lives.

We may not know whether it is God's will to heal a particular person in a given instance, but we can be sure that God wants to draw near to that person in the time of affliction; if someone is unsaved, we can be sure that God wants to draw them to himself. We can pray confidently for God's kingdom to come in the lives of individuals and for his will to be done, regardless of the temporal circumstances. To pray "kingdom prayers" for people is to directly invite God's presence into the lives of individuals in a way that he delights to answer.

If our hearts are focused on God's kingdom coming and his will being done in our lives, then we are free to pray the desires of our hearts. "Delight yourself in the LORD," the psalmist said, "and he will give you the desires of your heart" (Ps 37:4). Many understand this verse to mean not just that God will answer our prayer but also that he will actually place in our hearts the things he wants us to pray for. This idea is echoed in Jesus' statement in John 15:7: "If you remain in me and my words remain in you, ask whatever you wish, and it will be given you." We need not pray hesitantly, afraid to ask for something that might not be God's best; if our hearts are centered on him, he will answer our prayers in a way that accomplishes his will.

Jesus didn't add the phrase "if it is your will" to every petition in the Lord's Prayer. He had already submitted to the primacy of God's will at the beginning of the prayer, and thereafter prayed confidently for God's provision. In contrast, when Israel asked God, through Samuel, to provide a king for them, their hearts were clearly not God-focused. "Your kingdom come" was not what was on their minds; their main desire was to "be like all the other nations" (1 Sam 8:20). Though God made it clear through Samuel that this was not his will and even detailed many of the hardships they would suffer under an earthly king (1 Sam 8:11-18), the people persisted. God ultimately gave them what they asked for, and Israel did indeed become like the nations around them: war-torn, divided and idolatrous.

Not long after this, David became king and had it in his heart to build God a permanent dwelling place (2 Sam 7). The prophet Nathan gave him the go-ahead, but God had different plans. David was not the one to build the temple; his son would do it. Rather than chafe at God's "no," David praised God for promising him a son and an enduring kingdom. When our hearts are tuned in to God and we desire his will above all, he answers our prayers in ways that bring about his will. Perhaps this is what is meant by Proverbs 16:9: "In his heart a man plans his course, / but the LORD determines his steps." If our hearts are set on God, we may pray as we think best, and God will "correct" our direction whenever he needs to.

PAUL'S PRAYERS FOR THE CHURCHES

Some of the best examples of "kingdom prayers" can be found in the writings of Paul. Most of the churches to which Paul wrote were churches he had either founded or personally helped to grow. He was familiar with churches that lacked resources (2 Cor 8:1-3); certainly he knew of situations in the lives of those churches and of church members that needed prayer. Yet he did not focus his prayers on issues like these. Instead he consistently thanked God for the churches and individuals that he knew and prayed for God's spiritual blessings on them.

Paul thanked God for the Ephesians' faith and love (Eph 1:15); for the Philippians' partnership in the gospel (Phil 1:3-5); for the Colossians' faith and love (Col 1:3-5); for the Thessalonians' faith, love, works and endurance (1 Thess 1:2-3); and for Philemon's faith and love (Philem 4-5). Even the things for which Paul gave thanks were related to kingdom issues more than material blessings.

Consider the following requests that Paul made of God for various churches and individuals:

- For the Ephesians: wisdom, revelation, enlightenment, assurance of their hope and their inheritance and of God's power (Eph 1:17-19); power, Christ's indwelling their hearts, establishment in love, understanding of Christ's love, God's fullness (Eph 3:16-19)

- For the Philippians: completion of God's work in them, abundance of love, knowledge and insight, discernment, purity, righteousness and spiritual fruit (Phil 1:6-11)

- For the Colossians: knowledge of God's will, wisdom and understanding, spiritual fruit, strength and power, endurance, patience and joyful gratitude to God (Col 1:9-12)

- For Philemon: active witnessing, understanding of God's good gifts (Philem 6)

Paul's emphasis on kingdom issues in prayer serves as an example for us, both in private prayer and in community prayer. We should primarily be concerned with the coming of God's kingdom in the lives of those for whom we pray. This is part of what it means to see people through God's eyes.

With God All Things Are Possible

It is possible to pray for circumstances in such a way that God is left out of the equation. The distinction here is subtle (and in no way sinful), but the resulting focus can be significant.

Consider the following prayer: "Father, may there be peace in the Middle East." There is nothing wrong with the sentiment of this prayer, and certainly we can be sure that God prefers peace to war (although sometimes peace and justice are at odds with each other). But what are we asking God to do? Subtract the word *Father* and this prayer could be offered by someone who does not believe in a personal God.

In the Lord's Prayer, after general requests about God's kingdom and will, Jesus makes God the subject of all his petitions. He does not pray, "may we be fed," or "may we be forgiven," or "may we be protected," but he asks God directly to do all these things. In praying in that way, Jesus acknowledges the Father as the One who answers prayer and the Source of all we need.

How could we pray for God's intervention in the Middle East? Consider the following: "Father, please grant wisdom to the leaders of the countries in the Middle East. Enable them to put grudges and politics aside, and place in their hearts a strong desire for justice and peace. Please bring about reconciliation between those who have been enemies for generations." In these requests, God is acknowledged as the Source of everything that needs to happen in order to bring about peace in the region. This prayer illustrates the difference between praying simply that things will happen and really asking God to intervene in situations and in individuals' lives.

God is not restricted as to the prayers he can answer, and he's more than capable of figuring out how to intervene without our direct intercession. However, as we focus our prayers on God's intervention by asking him to do specific things, we acknowledge his sovereignty and strengthen our faith.

No Magic Formula

None of this should be taken to mean that there is some sort of "magic formula" for wording prayer. God delights in answering the prayers of a sincere heart, and he is not dependent on us to tell him exactly how to act. He knows the desires of our hearts (even before we express them), and he is completely sovereign to answer prayer in a way that honors him, even if we don't "word it" right.

That said, one of the great challenges of prayer in general and of community prayer in particular is to maintain a consistent focus on God. We've all heard the statement "prayer changes things," but actually, God changes things. He often chooses to do this in answer to prayer, and when we pray in a way that acknowledges that he is the One who answers, we honor him and remind ourselves that prayer is more about God than us.

We can help maintain this focus on God in several ways as we pray:

- by focusing our thoughts and prayers on the One who answers prayer rather than on the people and circumstances for which we pray
- by focusing our attention on those things that we know to be God's will

- by asking God directly to act and intervene, rather than praying generically that situations will change

If you pay attention to the wording of your prayers, focusing them on God, you will notice over time that your attitude toward prayer will shift and your understanding of God's sovereignty will increase. Prayer that is addressed to God, not to people, and that focuses on his kingdom and will, asking him directly to intervene, will honor God and draw you nearer to him.

QUESTIONS FOR DISCUSSION/REFLECTION

1. How does the phrase "hallowed be your name" set the context for your prayers?

2. When you ask for God's intervention in a situation, do you tend to pray generally or specifically? How might the phrases "your kingdom come, your will be done" affect the way you make requests of God?

3. What is the difference between saying "Prayer changes things" and "God changes things"? How does keeping the phrase "God changes things" in mind change your approach to prayer?

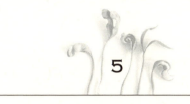

5

AGREEING IN PRAYER

I CAME HOME FROM THE Urbana Student Missions Convention with a passion to pray for God's kingdom to come around the world. My brother was one of the people in charge of planning Saturday evening vespers services at our church, so one Saturday the following summer I eagerly taught the gathered group about God's heart for the nations and about praying for the world. To personalize the message, I broke up the congregation into groups of three and four, and handed out cards with prayer requests for different countries—one card per person, each with seven or eight requests. The groups were to go off and pray for their countries and then come back together in about ten minutes.

As it happened, I ended up in a group with my brother and my father. I opened the prayer time by praying for the country on my card. By the time I was done praying, the entire ten minutes had been used up! Neither my brother or my father got a chance to pray. Afterward, my father told me,

"That was an interesting service, but that kind of prayer is not for me."

I learned an important lesson that day. Being "together in prayer" means much more than simply praying in the same place at the same time with other believers. There is an implied unity of heart and mind, a sense of common purpose and vision, and a mutual submission that encourages everyone in the group to participate.

The early church experienced this kind of deep unity and mutual submission to an extent that is hard to picture in Western culture today. Part of this unity had a geographical element—the believers were located close to each other and met together often (Acts 1:14; 2:1, 46; 4:23; 5:12). Another part of the unity came from their shared vision that Jesus was the Messiah and their determination to make him known (Acts 2; 4:1-2; 5:12-16, 42). They shared a concern for each other that led them to voluntarily provide for the needy among them (Acts 2:45; 4:32-36). They resolved problems in a way that promoted unity rather than division (Acts 6:1-7). In so many ways, the early believers were "one in heart and mind" (Acts 4:32). Through all of these early chapters of Acts, we see a thread of community prayer responding to and enhancing this unity (Acts 1:14; 2:42; 4:24).

Much of Western society today is based on a social and economic model that mostly precludes the type of community living that the early church experienced. We can hardly imagine what it would be like to be in the temple courts together daily, eating together regularly (Acts 2:46) or truly devoting our lives to things like scriptural teaching and fellowship (Acts 2:42). But it is still possible to experience a level of unity that enables group members to pray as one, seeking God's agenda and not their own. This unity is the basis for Jesus' promise in Matthew 18:19-20: "If two of you on earth agree about anything you ask for, it will be done for you by my Father in heaven. For where two or three come together in my name, there am I with them."

The idea of being "together" has to do with more than just physical proximity; it also has to do with agreement. It is not enough to simply meet together and pray; the idea is to be "together in prayer." This is what most distinguishes the community prayer time from the private prayer time; without agreement, group members are better off simply praying on their own.

Agreeing in prayer gives us the opportunity to experience a level of community and fellowship that is not possible in private prayer. Truly agreeing together in prayer is the fulfillment that most prayer groups are crying out for and too few are experiencing. Making God the focus of our prayers by addressing him and not others in the group, and seeking his will and kingdom and not our own agenda—these bring agreement within the group. In this chapter, we will examine briefly how these same practices help promote unity and agreement in prayer. We'll then look at a couple more prayer practices that can help a group pray together more effectively.

FOCUSING ON GOD

We've already seen how addressing people in prayer can cause others in our group to feel preached to and to become defensive or discouraged. Prayer for me to be more seeker-focused or a better financial steward or more forgiving is likely to leave me feeling guilty rather than encouraged. I may indeed need to be all those things (and more), but as I hear other people express my failings in prayer, my ability to truly enter into those prayers and agree with them is greatly diminished. On the other hand, prayer that asks God to move in my life by changing me or by changing my circumstances is much more likely to result in my agreement and even participation.

Similarly, prayers that advance a particular agenda can actually divide, rather than unite, a group. It doesn't take long for a prayer time to degenerate when people are praying with competing agendas. They may be well-intentioned and heartfelt, but they destroy the possibility of agreement.

The church I attend is a relatively new regional campus for an existing church, and one of the groups I pray with was praying from the perspective that every church member who lives in our area should leave the parent church and come help with the church plant. This was an assumption I never agreed with. So I was never able to pray in agreement. When I confronted the group, some members couldn't understand my concern and continued to pray in the same way. Eventually, due to divisions within the ministry, they were asked by our director to leave the team. Though agenda-based praying doesn't always lead to such an extreme result, it can be an indication of deeper unity issues in the group and should be addressed overtly.

Picture a church staff praying over the coming year's budget. Everyone present realizes that the budget itself is a zero-sum game: more money to one area necessarily means less money to other areas. A staff member who prays specifically that God will increase funding for a particular ministry is therefore almost necessarily praying that the budget for other areas will be reduced. How ought the staff to pray? If everyone comes to the staff prayer time with an open heart and open hands, willing to let God emphasize those ministries that he deems important (even to the detriment of others), it becomes much easier to pray in ways that will promote unity and agreement. Freed from agendas related to specific ministries, staff members can focus in prayer on the good of the congregation, on honoring God's name in ministry, on serving the community.

FOCUSING ON EACH OTHER

Have you ever had a conversation with someone who clearly was not listening to you but rather just waiting for their chance to speak? Nearly all of us have experienced this at one time or another, and we know the disappointment of having someone care so little about what's on our mind that they don't even acknowledge our topic but immediately move on to their own. Multiple people "conversing" in this way don't produce a real conversation but rather a series of monologues. Similarly, a community prayer time where each person focuses on their own topic without reference to the prayers of others isn't really community prayer at all; it's more of a series of individual prayers. True agreement in prayer requires that we understand the group dynamics of community prayer and participate accordingly.

Agreeing in prayer requires that we listen to the person praying and enter into that person's prayers. Some people express agreement with a whispered "Amen" or other phrase.

Others express it by praying silently along with the one who is praying aloud. In these ways, the group is actually praying together and the one praying aloud can be thought of as simply taking the lead.

One way to help the group agree in prayer is to focus the prayer time on a central theme. Several group members pray on the same topic in turn, each one focusing on a particular aspect of the topic. At first, this may seem limiting. After all, just how long can you pray for topic X before running out of things to pray? Actually, it's surprising how much more deeply we can pray for a topic when we make that topic the focus of our prayer time. Even a group seasoned in praying together will have a hard time staying focused in a prayer time whose topics vary from personal needs to church requests to national issues to missionaries and so on. Keeping the time focused builds excitement, agreement and momentum, and is also more likely to result in group members continuing to pray on their own for the topic covered. If your prayer is one of praise, focus on one attribute of God rather than running through an entire litany. If the group is focusing on a time of intercession for missionaries, then pray for only one at a time. If you are praying for one another in the group, pray for one person at a time. You might be surprised at how such focused prayer can turn out to be a real vision-casting time in the minds of group members.

Another way to help focus the group in prayer is to encourage group members to pray brief, direct prayers on a single topic. Such prayer, as we will see, promotes participation and agreement. And yet, as simple and important as this is, brief, focused prayer can be one of the hardest practices to follow consistently.

Lengthy prayers are one of the biggest discouragements to group members in terms of their own participation. No one wants to follow the lengthy prayer; subconsciously, we know that we will not "measure up" to a long, eloquent discourse. This is a natural dynamic of praying together. Meanwhile, the lengthy prayer communicates to the group that the one praying is not interested in the participation of others. Just as the person who dominates a conversation reveals a lack of interest in what others have to say, the pray-er who dominates the prayer time elevates his or her own contribution over that of others. Such an environment discourages agreement and unity within the group. A lengthy prayer might jump from topic to topic or else so saturate a given topic that others in the group have nothing further to add. How do you follow the person who just prayed about everything? You don't. The message communicated is that others in the group have no meaningful contribution to make to the prayer time.

Lengthy prayer thus tends to cause group members to disengage, rather than to participate. God has a long attention span; people do not. As Brother Lawrence wrote in his classic *The Practice of the Presence of God,* "It isn't necessary to be too verbose in prayer, because lengthy prayers encourage wandering thoughts." If that's true of the person praying, how much more is it true of those listening!

Not all lengthy, rambling prayers come from hearts wrong before God, of course. The lengthy prayers that Jesus condemned were intended for people, not for God. Nonetheless,

Jesus discouraged lengthy prayers because God already knows what we need (Mt 6). He doesn't need much information and he doesn't need to be cajoled into acting. He simply wants us to entrust the situation to his care. Jesus applauded a tax collector's brief, sincere prayer in Luke 18:9-14. He taught the very brief prayer in Matthew 6 as a model for how his followers should pray. Praying briefly encourages the contributions of others. Brief, focused prayer helps others in the group to "pray alongside" silently with the one who is praying out loud, fostering agreement in prayer. Brief prayer leaves room for others to participate and leads to groupwide involvement, rather than the disengagement that character-izes prayer times dominated by lengthy prayer.

Brief prayer precludes many of the ways in which people address one another, rather than God, in prayer. The one praying focuses on making simple requests of God rather than praying all around a given topic. Community prayer is not like creative writing; no bonus points are awarded for how well a situation is described. In fact, "togetherness" points are subtracted. If you find yourself using explanatory words, like *because,* or numerous adjectives, you're probably adding details that you don't need to.

> **TIP:** *If you find yourself using explanatory words, like* because, *or numerous adjectives, you're probably adding details you don't need to.*

One of the best ways to help a group develop a prayer around a topic together is by inviting group members to pray briefly on a given topic multiple times. This helps reduce the need to "cover it all" in one prayer. Remember too that God knows our needs before we ask him. What if, in your group's diligence to pray briefly, you forget to mention a particular aspect of a topic that you wanted to pray about? Good news: God is capable of answering not only the prayers we verbalize but also the prayers that are in our hearts—prayers we haven't even thought of yet! So don't feel compelled to completely cover a topic as you pray. God hears and answers the unspoken prayer as well as the spoken one.

During a time of sharing requests, a group member mentions Harry, a close friend of one of the group members (but not a member of the group himself) who has just found out that he has cancer. As the group heads to prayer, the first person to pray for Harry starts off praying for God's peace for Harry and for a sense of God's comforting presence. The second person then extends that prayer to cover Harry's family and asks for wisdom in the decisions that lie ahead. The third person prays for the surgery and for wisdom for the doctors. Someone else prays for Harry's recovery from the surgery. The prayer goes on from there. Each prayer is brief, focused on one aspect of the topic. In this way, the whole group participates together in praying for Harry, and each one contributes meaningfully to the group prayer. Each member develops a sense of ownership in what is being prayed for Harry. The members track with each other's prayers and participate together in the conversation with God. They are of one heart and mind.

QUESTIONS FOR DISCUSSION/REFLECTION

1. Have you ever prayed in a group where you could sense

significant agreement? significant disagreement? What do you think contributed to the level of agreement or disagreement?

2. Talk about a time you experienced Brother Lawrence's observation that "lengthy prayers encourage wandering thoughts."

6

LEADING EFFECTIVE
COMMUNITY PRAYER

EFFECTIVE COMMUNITY PRAYER ULTIMATELY leads to a group growing in closeness to God. As a group focuses on God's kingdom and his will in prayer, he reveals himself to them (Jer 29:12-13). In turn, as God reveals his will more and more to the group, members increasingly tend to pray kingdom prayers for each other and for other people and situations. The focus in prayer evolves from temporal circumstances to the types of kingdom prayers that Paul prayed for the New Testament churches.

As the group continues to pray kingdom prayers for each other, members develop more Christlike character. Increasingly, the group is able to discern God's heart in the situations they pray for. The group learns to rejoice in God's answers to prayer, whatever form those answers take. With Paul, they are able to rejoice in God's "Yes" and "No," learning to be content whatever the circumstances. At the same time, group members are encouraged to expect God's answers and to see him at work in the world and in their lives. The group grows in faith and trust in God, furthering the development of the community relationship with God.

Ultimately, God's answers to prayer—both for group members and for people and circumstances outside the group—lead the group to a growing sense of participation in the work God is doing in their lives and in the world. A feeling of partnership with God develops, further building up the group's relationship with God.

The Goal: Growing in Closeness

As the group grows closer to God, the natural result is an increasing sense of unity. The group finds common ground as together they seek God's will and experience his presence in prayer. The sense of participation in God's work through prayer builds a common sense of purpose. But effective community prayer also contributes directly to the experience of unity, as the horizontal dimension of prayer is carefully cultivated.

As a group learns to listen to each other and develops a cohesive conversation with God during their prayer time, rather than a progression of unrelated monologues, everyone's contribution is valued. People are encouraged to participate, and unity grows. Rather than being intimidated by lengthy, eloquent prayers, group members are given confidence to participate together in brief, connected prayers. When both of these practices are followed, a sense of participating together in a common mission develops.

Community prayer cannot accomplish these things on its

own, however. Unity comes to a group through shared experiences, such as service events, vision trips or retreats, as well as times of prayer together. Shared Bible study is needed for the group to grow over the long term in its relationship with God. A common sense of mission draws a group together and adds a sense of urgency to the prayer time.

My best experiences of community prayer were in college, with the leadership team of our InterVarsity chapter. We shared many service experiences, participated in small group Bible studies and often met together for prayer. Our mission—making disciples on campus—drew the group together and added urgency to our prayers.

One spring, just after school was out, several of us went up to Cedar Campus, an InterVarsity retreat center in northern Michigan, for what would be the first of many chapter camps that our group attended. We were newcomers to this type of leadership experience, and we faced many challenges that week, both personal and corporate, that we had not anticipated. I recall one particular planning session in which we could not arrive at a consensus regarding direction for the coming year, no matter how hard we tried or how many different ideas we discussed. Although we were a close group, tensions ran a bit high as we left that session with issues that we knew were still hanging over us. There were several strong leaders in our group, making it even more difficult to reach an agreement.

During our break, a couple of us decided that we would open our next session with a prolonged period of time in prayer. We scrapped our agenda for the session (though we were already behind schedule) and earnestly sought the Lord in prayer. By the time we were done, we had such a sense of clarity from God that we wondered what our problem could have been. Even now, over twenty years later, I remember the sweetness of our fellowship together—all centered around a strong community prayer life. One of the staff even commented to us as we served in the kitchen together that we were one of the most united leadership teams he had ever seen.

On another occasion I was in a Bible study track, learning about and practicing inductive Bible study. I don't remember the passage we were studying, but at one point I came into a fairly sharp disagreement with another member of the group over the interpretation of a particular portion of the passage. Years have dimmed the details, but I remember being concerned about the integrity of our study methods. Over lunch, I asked my chapter mates to pray with me regarding this issue because I was so bothered by the disunity of the study and concerned over truly understanding the passage. We had a great time of prayer together, but I still went back to the study a little apprehensive. As it turned out, I needn't have been; whatever the disagreement had been, it seemed that God had put both of us on the same page and we were able to move on as a group with a common understanding of the passage. I don't remember if I saw it her way or if she saw it my way (or if we both saw it a completely different way), but I do remember that our disagreement of the morning vanished as though it had never been.

Not all community prayer will be answered so quickly or so obviously, of course, but I mention these examples as an illustration of all that community prayer can be when practiced effectively. Community prayer is an important part of the church's life as the body of Christ, but how do we lead our groups into a dynamic community prayer life, especially if they do not yet have the same vision for community prayer that we do? How do we help a small group grow in its practice of community prayer? The steps outlined in this chapter should help you take your group into a more vibrant practice of praying together.

GETTING STARTED: CASTING A VISION

One of the tasks of a small group leader is to help the group grow in prayer. This will look different for different types of groups, of course. The group that is primarily a serving team will have limited time for anything but their task. The group that is a discipleship group will have much more time for prayer. The seeker group will have a completely different prayer dynamic and may not even have a time of true community prayer like we've been discussing; after all, community prayer assumes that the community already believes in the God to whom they are praying. How can a group that struggles to pray together grow in this area? How can a group that doesn't pray together start?

Community prayer is not the group leader's idea. It's not my idea either; it comes from Scripture. A meaningful vision for community prayer must therefore start with our ultimate authority, God's Word. The following summary of passages shows how the early church in Acts depended on prayer and specifically on community prayer.

- Acts 1:14   The believers joined together constantly in prayer.

- Acts 1:23-26 The disciples prayed together before choosing a replacement for Judas.

- Acts 2:42   The believers devoted themselves to prayer, among other things. The context shows this to be community prayer.
- Acts 4:23-31   The believers joined together in prayer on the release of Peter and John.
- Acts 6:4   The apostles gave their attention to prayer and the ministry of the word; again, in context, this was likely community prayer.
- Acts 12:5, 12   The church prayed earnestly (and apparently for a period of time) for Peter's release from prison.
- Acts 13:3   The church at Antioch sent off Paul and Barnabas on their missionary journey in the context of prayer and fasting.
- Acts 16:25   Paul and Silas had a two-person prayer and worship time in prison.
- Acts 20:36   Paul prayed with the Ephesian elders as he headed toward Jerusalem.

Elsewhere in the New Testament the church is commanded to pray in community:

- Mt 18:19-20   Jesus instructed his followers to pray together.
- Jas 5:16   James commands us to confess our sins to each other and to pray for each other.

Community prayer will bring several benefits to your group, and you may need to make the group aware of these as part of casting a vision.

- Faith will be built as you see God answer your prayers.

- Unity will be built as you pray for one another.

- God will be lifted up as the focus of your group as you address him in prayer.

- The group will be empowered to grow in their personal prayer lives.

Community prayer is not just a benefit but also a safeguard for your group members. If there is resistance in your group to developing a community prayer life, then you would do them a favor to challenge them each with this question: "Who in your life knows you well enough and is committed enough to you that they watchfully pray for you on a regular basis?" If your group members all have people praying for them, that's great (and very unusual). But if not, then your community needs to become a community of prayer for its own members.

STEP 1: WHERE ARE YOU?

It's important that you understand the level of comfort and experience that each group member has in both personal and group prayer in order to help your group grow in this area. Do you have some seasoned "prayer warriors" who have prayed in many group settings before? Do you have some people who have never prayed in a group before? Do you have people who don't really know how to relate to God in a conversational style?

If your group is at different places in their understanding and experience of prayer, or if you don't really know where each member is in their own personal prayer life, then it might be helpful to spend a few weeks on a Bible study regarding prayer. There are many good studies available on the topic of prayer, and spending some time on this topic will help you understand the beliefs and experience of each of your group members. It may also help clear up some misconceptions that members have about prayer and thus lay a strong foundation for biblical prayer in a community setting.

If you need to, spend some one-on-one time with each group member around the topic of prayer, specifically community prayer. This can be helpful if your group has never prayed together before or if you have noticed certain problems in your group prayer times. Do you have a person who consistently dominates the prayer time and ends up intimidating other, less experienced group members? Perhaps you could meet with that person and enlist their help in getting others to participate more by dialing back on their own prayer participation.

STEP 2: CREATE A SAFE PLACE

Once you have an understanding of where each group member is in their prayer life, then it's time to begin. Even if your group has been praying together for a while, you may need to make a sort of "new beginning." Create an atmosphere in which people will open up to share important personal prayer needs. Put group members at ease with community prayer by setting expectations clearly and removing any "performance pressure" they may feel. The safer people feel with the group, the more they will participate in group prayer time.

The first step toward helping the group open up in prayer is to ensure the absolute confidentiality of all prayer requests and prayers shared within the group. If your group has been praying together for some time, everyone probably under-stands this already. But if you have people who are new in the group or if your group is new to praying together, you need to make this explicit. Unless the member gives specific permission otherwise, what is shared in the group needs to stay in the group. Even if you don't pray together, your group has probably developed some level of trust over the time of meeting together. Making this trust explicit will help group members feel safer in prayer.

Remove performance pressure by assuring the group that it is not necessary for each person to pray aloud. Silent prayer is perfectly acceptable as a way of participating in the com-munity prayer. Unless you are sure that everyone is comfort-able praying aloud and is prepared to participate that way, avoid exercises that require each person to pray aloud, par-ticularly the dreaded "circle prayer" where the group goes round in a circle, each person praying along some guided topic. Such a practice will make those who are uncomfort-able with community prayer even more uncomfortable. In-stead of truly entering into the prayers of others in the group and agreeing silently with them, such members will be sweating out the time until their "turn" comes, hoping against hope that their prayer will turn out okay (whatever that means). Group members in this position will feel no community in the prayer time; instead, they will feel isolated and pressured. They will come to dread the prayer time.

Assure your group that times of silence are okay. Ideally, listening to God should be part of your prayer experience together, and it's hard to listen to God if someone is always talking. There is a time and a place to "be still, and know that I am God" (Ps 46:10). However, unless you've mentioned it, some group members will become very uncomfortable during times of silence and will feel compelled to fill them with prayer. Such a compulsion is just as uncomfortable as the "circle prayer" mentioned above, and disrupts a person's sense of community. You'll need to use your judgment, of course, as to how much silence is good and what point group members may have just "tuned out" and need to be brought back to focusing on God.

Don't be afraid to lead the time clearly and to communicate expectations explicitly. Group members who are new to community prayer will be much more comfortable if they know what to expect beforehand. Instruct the group about keeping prayers brief, sticking to one topic, praying as a group through one topic before moving on to the next, keeping God as the focus of the prayers and so on. You don't need to spend a lot of time on this, but short reminders will be helpful to get everyone on the same page. Also, if you have communicated beforehand the expectation that prayers will be brief and focused; then you free group members to follow a long, winding prayer with a short one without feeling like they will be looked down on for not being eloquent.

STEP 3: CLARIFY THE LOGISTICS

If your group is new to praying together, you may need to clarify some logistical issues. For example, how will the group know when the prayer time is over? How will each member know when the person praying is finished? You can remove fears that group members may have about "prayer faux pas" by communicating these things up front.

It's always good to be clear about who will open and who will close the prayer time. Choose a person before you begin your prayer time for each of these prayer "slots." For groups that have been together for some time and are comfortable praying together, it's probably okay to ask a couple of people to fill these slots on the spot. For groups that are new to praying together or that have people at different levels of experience and comfort, a better practice would be to ask people in advance (and in private) if they would play these roles. Either way, be sure that the group knows who will be opening and closing the prayer time.

The "opening" prayer is important because it turns the group's focus to God. Often, the opening prayer will set the tone and the pace for the entire prayer time. If it is long and winding, other group members will imitate those characteristics; if it is brief and God-centered, others will also pray in that style. One great way to focus the group's attention on God at the beginning is to open with a time of praise or thanksgiving.

The "closing" slot is also very important. A brief summary of what has been lifted up to God in prayer may be appropriate. Focusing on his sovereignty and placing trust in him to answer all the prayers offered in his time and in his way ensures that the group will leave with their hearts and minds on God. The "closer" needs to have a sense of when the group is finished praying—an idea of when the topics for prayer have all been covered. Typically, a prolonged silence will indicate that the group is ready to close, but it can take some experience to make that judgment. Consequently, it is important that the people who are praying in these places know how to open or close a prayer meeting. If you are not comfortable assigning these spots to someone else in the group, then it's perfectly fine for you as the leader to open and close the time.

How long is "long enough" for a group to pray together? The answer to that question varies with the group, the topics being prayed for and how each group member is feeling at that particular time. If your group is new to prayer, don't push for an extended time of prayer together. You'd be surprised how long ten to fifteen minutes can be for a group that's never prayed together before. On the other hand, if the group is still going strong and is obviously communing together in prayer, don't cut it off too early.

Avoid having the prayer time at the end of your group's time together, particularly if the group has a set time for meeting. You want to honor the group's meeting times by not going beyond the stated ending time. That can sometimes mean a very abbreviated prayer time, particularly if you have used more time than you thought you would for other group activities. If you're really serious about growing your group in prayer, and if you have stated beginning and ending times for the group meeting, consider making prayer the first thing you do together instead of the last thing. This frees the group to spend extra time in prayer if there is a particular need. It also allows God room to modify the meeting's agenda if needed (say, if something comes up as a prayer request that the group feels a need to address further).

Another logistical issue in community prayer is knowing when one group member is finished praying so that another may start. Often groups that have been praying together for some time simply rely on silence as an indicator that a group member is finished, but this is not always a reliable method. One suggestion for groups newer to community prayer is to have each member finish each turn with the phrase "in Jesus' name." This common phrase for ending times of personal prayer can be used to indicate that a person has completed praying for the current topic.

BEGINNING THE TIME: SET THE FOCUS

Your group's prayer time will be far more dynamic and will develop greater agreement if you focus the time on a particular subject. This subject could be personal prayer requests or it could be something outside the group, such as your church or neighborhood, or possibly missionaries you know or countries where the church is under persecution. Obviously, the number of topics available for prayer is pretty much limitless; thus, you need to set some sort of topical "boundaries" for your time in prayer. This does not mean that you can pray for only one subject in your prayer time, but you should be clear about what subjects you are praying for and how you will transition from one subject to another.

Unless your small group has adopted a "mission" to pray for a particular subject area, most of your prayer time will probably be spent praying for each other. This is perfectly appropriate; in fact, there's a good chance that, for most of the people in your group, the people most committed to praying specifically for them will be the members of your group. Because of this, even groups who have a particular prayer emphasis outside the group should also spend some time praying for each other.

Once you have determined and communicated the subject

area(s) for your group's prayer time, you need a way of sharing the information that will be used for prayer. If the subject of the prayer time will be personal prayer requests, then you will need to spend some time sharing these requests before going to prayer. The sharing of personal prayer requests can be one of the most problematic aspects of praying together, for many reasons. For more details on leading this time, see chapter seven.

If your group's prayer time is going to focus on something other than the group members' prayer requests, then you need to put that information in front of the group in a way that will help them to pray. Some people pray better from lists than others do, but if you're going to keep the time focused, you need some sort of visual aid that people can refer to as they pray. If you're praying for the church's missionaries, for example, you might prepare a list of a few prayer requests for each missionary, then pray for one missionary at a time. If you're going to have a "world events" prayer time, don't just say, "We're going to pray for world events now"; instead, come with a list of events and situations that need prayer, and focus the time on those. Ask group members if they have anything else (related to the subject area) that they'd like to pray for, and have everyone add those items to their lists. Give group members time to read through the lists and to ask any questions that they might have.

Whatever your subject areas will be, make sure that the group knows what to pray for and how the prayer time will progress. Communicating this in advance helps set expectations for the group. Some group members may feel a bit "limited" by focusing prayer on one or two subject areas, but this is truly the best way to build agreement and participation in community prayer (as opposed to skipping through many subjects). If it's appropriate for your group, you can help group members take ownership of this time by asking them in turn to come up with the subject area and to provide prayer materials for a given group meeting. This way, if your group members have any particular passions for prayer, you can make sure that you are providing opportunities to pray in those areas.

Environment: Tailoring the Prayer Time to Your Group

So far, we have discussed leading the group in prayer in terms of the logistics. Community prayer is not a "one size fits all" endeavor, however. The actual working out of prayer practices will look different for different groups. We'll look at a couple of types of groups in this section.

Serving teams. If your group is primarily a serving team and the majority of your time is devoted to the task, then prayer time for you will look very different from that of a group primarily devoted to Bible study or prayer. Community prayer is particularly important, though also particularly difficult, for serving teams. Your time limitations dictate in large part how deep your community prayer time will be, and your physical surroundings may not be conducive to focusing a time in prayer together.

Community prayer is important enough for your group that it's worth overcoming such obstacles to achieve. If you're willing to be a bit creative and flexible, your group can still experience and grow in community prayer despite the time and environmental limitations. First, decide on a time in your group's schedule that would be best for community prayer. It doesn't need to be a lengthy time, and there's no intrinsic reason why it should be in a particular time slot (beginning, middle, end); make this decision based on the logistics of your group. If people come at different times to begin their serving but all leave at the same time, then maybe prayer at the end would be most appropriate. If people all arrive at the same time but leave at different times, you might want to consider using the first few minutes for prayer. If the logistics support it, you might have a brief time of prayer at the beginning of your serving time regarding the task and the group's service, then a second brief time of prayer at the end interceding for various group members. If there is a break in the middle of your serving time, you might consider that time for prayer.

Our church's ushers and greeters gather for a time of prayer before each service. The musicians also have a brief prayer time in the "green room" before going onstage. Other teams, however, are more challenged to find a time and place where they can pray together around their serving time.

If the group's serving schedule or environment simply doesn't permit a time for the whole group to pray, you still have some alternatives. If group members are open to the idea, you might consider setting up a time entirely separate from your serving time for the group to meet and pray together. Or you might set up prayer partners or trios who can take time to pray together before, during or after your serving time.

If you persevere, God will bring about a community prayer

life that is pleasing to him. He is not holding you accountable for time you do not have together; he simply wants to be the focus of the time you do have. Whenever you do pray together, it's particularly important for you to make sure that the focus of the prayer time is on God, not on the task you're performing. This doesn't mean that you shouldn't pray about the task, but serving teams tend to be particularly task-oriented, so this may be a tougher challenge for you than it is for other types of groups. There's a difference, however, between praying about something and focusing prayer on that something, between asking God to act ("Father, welcome people to church today through our traffic team") and describing a concern ("May people be safe as they enter our parking lot today and may they feel welcome").

Seeker groups. Seeker groups are called by many different names, but they're all meant to be a safe place for nonbelievers to investigate the claims of Christ and to be exposed to the gospel. Typically, such a group has a mix of believers and nonbelievers in it. If you lead such a group, the "rules" are entirely different for you than for leaders of other group types. Community prayer is not necessarily irrelevant to your group, but it will have a different focus and probably take a different form than in believers' groups.

You already realize that you can't make assumptions about what your group members might or might not believe. This applies also to prayer. Perhaps some of them have never prayed before, particularly in a group setting. Some have been exposed to prayer at some point, but you probably don't know what their experience was like, unless it has been a topic of discussion in your group.

If most people in your group don't believe in prayer, then it may not be a good idea to insist on a time of group prayer in your meetings. Have a discussion about it and get your group members' input. Once you know where they stand, you'll have a better idea how to proceed. You might want to try to propose prayer as kind of an "experiment"—a way for group members to see if God is really there and if he really does care. This can be a bit faith-stretching and risky, since God does not always answer prayer in the way we envision. But if you're up for it, ask each group member (particularly the nonbelievers) to identify an area in his or her life in which God's intervention is especially needed. Then get the group to agree to pray together for that area and to pray while apart also. This could actually be a great way to bring non-believers to Christ, as they see how God answers prayer for "even them."

If you're going to pray together as a group, it is particularly important in seeker small groups to avoid "God talk" and keep prayers brief and to the point. Interestingly, it's most likely not the nonbelievers in your group who will have a problem with this; it's most likely the believers. Be sure that the believers in the group understand the importance of making the prayer time one in which nonbelievers will feel comfortable participating.

Every believer was once a nonbeliever who had a prayer answered. At some point in time, God answered that person's prayer for forgiveness and salvation, changing the nonbeliever's heart into a heart of belief and faith. God is in the business of answering prayers of nonbelievers as a means of drawing them to him.

If it's your sense that the nonbelievers in your group aren't particularly open to praying together, you can still enjoy community prayer with the other believers in the group, either before or after your group time, or perhaps at some other time. It's particularly important that you pray with the other believers in the group specifically for the salvation of the seekers, and community prayer is a great way to do that.

Discipleship groups. Discipleship groups, focused on Bible study, have a couple of advantages over the other two types of groups. The expectations of your group members are probably conducive to community prayer (as opposed to the expectations in a seeker group, for example), and your time is more at your own disposal than is the case for a serving team.

These advantages don't automatically translate to a successful community prayer life, however, and there can still be some significant hurdles to overcome. Some of them have to do with community prayer in general. But other challenges may come from various places. Your meeting place, for example, may not be conducive to a time of community prayer. If you meet in a restaurant, as one of my small groups does, then you know it can be pretty much impossible to devote significant time to prayer in that setting.

Sometimes it may be necessary to think "outside the box" in terms of having community prayer time together. One possibility might be to have your group meet occasionally in the house of one of your group members and devote that time to prayer. Another might be to see if smaller "groups"— perhaps even just two or three people at a time—could get together to pray. Community prayer can happen wherever two or more are gathered in Jesus' name.

MOVING TOWARD COMMUNITY PRAYER

Most of the suggestions in this chapter have assumed that your group is not accustomed to praying together regularly as a significant part of your group life. The idea here has been to help you move into community prayer in a way that will be comfortable for group members and will result in an effective community prayer life together. But what if your group is not open to the idea of community prayer? What if logistical concerns prevent you from praying together significantly? There are still some steps you can take to move in the direction of community prayer, even if you can't experience it fully.

If your group is not open to praying together regularly, the first thing to do is to ask yourself why that's the case. Is it a lack of vision for prayer? Is it a lack of trust? Is it a fear of increased accountability? Do people in the group fear what others might think of their prayers? Is the intimacy level in the group not what it needs to be for a significant community prayer life?

Community prayer is intended to be a regular, significant part of the life of the body of Christ. If there is something in your group that is preventing that from happening, you need to identify and address it. As you are doing that, there are a few other first steps you might take to move in the direction of community prayer without implementing a full-blown group prayer time.

If the problem is lack of vision, then the place to start is probably with the Scriptures. Develop some Bible studies around the passages in Acts (or others that you know of) and use them as your study together. And, of course, you need to be in prayer personally that God will spread the vision for community prayer in your group.

If the problem is more along the lines of lack of trust or intimacy or perhaps fear of accountability, then one possible solution would be to set up prayer partnerships. This way, people don't have to trust the whole group with their prayer concerns; they can share those with just one other person. Depending on the group, you might want to set up permanent prayer partnerships or rotate them after a specific period of time. Remember, however, that prayer partnerships are not an "icebreaker" activity. Don't force together people who are not comfortable with each other.

If you set up prayer partnerships, you could either allot time during the group for people to pray with their partners, or you could set that up to take place outside of group time, for example, with prayer cards. If you set up the prayer time to take place outside of group time, then you may want to occasionally ask the group how the prayer partnerships are going, as a way for you to keep track of how effective they are.

Another possibility if trust or intimacy is the problem is to set up your prayer time initially as "mission." Rather than praying for each other, use the time to focus on a topic of interest to the group. Examples might include prayer for the church, for the nation, for unreached peoples around the world and so on. You could even rotate the topics from time to time. This will get your group used to praying together without requiring that they share personal details.

Ultimately, however, if trust remains an issue in your group over a long period of time (rather than just a "getting to know you" issue), this is something you'll need to address. Leaving the topic of prayer aside for a moment, you can't build community over a long period of time with people who will not trust each other and ultimately open their lives up to one another.

Whatever intermediate steps you choose, remember to be in constant prayer for God to address whatever issues are keeping you from a full community prayer life. Ask him to break down whatever barriers are in the way and to lead the group into meaningful, significant prayer together. This is a prayer he will delight to answer, and he may even do some significant work in your group members' hearts in the process.

QUESTIONS FOR DISCUSSION/REFLECTION

1. Which of the following best describes where your group is in community prayer?

   a. The group prays together regularly and effectively.

   b. The group prays together regularly but not all that effectively.

   c. The group doesn't pray together regularly but would be open to the idea.

   d. There's not much interest in community prayer in the group.

2. Are all your group members "on the same page" when it comes to community prayer? If not, what can you do to promote a common understanding?

3. If your group is not currently praying together, was there any particular step toward community prayer discussed in this chapter that might help move your group in that direction?

7

PRAYING FOR ONE ANOTHER

"Does anyone have any prayer requests?" Thus begins what is often the most dreaded time of any small group meeting. Mary's Aunt Gertrude is in the hospital again, and explaining her condition requires a minimum of fifteen minutes (each time). John really needs some prayer but is afraid to open up to the group and express his deep needs. Tim is anxious to get going; the Bible study is over and he never did really get the point of this "sharing and prayer" time. Karen is frustrated because the group always seems to spend all its time talking and not much time in prayer. Joe, the leader, knows he needs to incorporate prayer in his small group but senses the group's disconnectedness and lack of vision for praying together.

Have you ever been any of the above people? If so, the frustration you've experienced is not unusual; in fact, it's a normal part of the way many groups pray together. If you've been tempted to give up on prayer in your small group as a result of situations like the one above, don't! Praying effectively for one another in a group setting is worth the time and effort it takes for your group to learn to do it well. As you and your group members lift each other up in prayer, you usher one another into the very presence of God and invite his work in your lives. You submit to him, both as individuals and as a group, and nothing builds more powerful community than seeking God together for one another.

SET THE TONE

One of the most difficult areas to handle regarding group prayer can be the sharing of prayer requests. If the group is going to be praying for one another, then it is imperative to provide a time for sharing information about the requests before going to prayer; otherwise, the prayer time itself will be spent sharing information rather than focusing on God. However, leading the time of sharing can require both discernment and courage.

On the one extreme, there may be some group members who are reluctant to open up enough to share anything personal (this is often revealed by consistent requests for prayer for family members or friends rather than for themselves). This will hinder the group in praying for them, and will slow the development of real community in prayer. On the other extreme, there may be some members who feel that they need to give a full biography in order to share a prayer need.

> **TIP:** *Manage the time of sharing prayer requests carefully to keep from getting sidetracked.*

Somewhere in the middle is what you're shooting for.

Set the tone for the sharing time by emphasizing that your purpose is to invite God's supernatural presence into the lives of each of the group members and to request his answers to prayer. The sharing of requests is not an end in itself but rather a means to the end of approaching God in prayer and inviting his intervention. Naturally, some situations will require more explanation than others. You need to give room for enough information to be shared that the group will be able to pray intelligently about situations in the lives of group members. But you also need to be discerning to know when the line has been crossed and the sharing is drawing the focus away from God.

As with many situations involving prayer, there are no hard-and-fast rules about how much time to allow for sharing. If your group does this regularly, then you will need less time than if you do it only occasionally, because group members will naturally be more updated on each others' lives. Be careful to avoid turning the sharing time into a counseling session. The one sharing may indeed need counseling or other next steps, but the point of the sharing time is to bring the situations before God. Your group may not even be qualified to guide the person through those next steps. Be sensitive to situations that may call for more than prayer, and suggest that you begin by praying over the situation, then pursuing other next steps as appropriate.

ENCOURAGE PERSONAL SHARING
Within the guidelines of managing the time, encourage group members to share personal requests. Some group

members may tend to share only requests for others. This can be a symptom of lack of trust or intimacy in the group, or it can be a means of avoiding accountability. Group members will more readily relate to praying for one another than for others whom they will most likely never meet. Interest and involvement in prayer is easier to maintain when group members focus primarily on their own needs.

As with other guidelines, this is not a prohibition against praying for family or friends outside the group. Occasionally, a significant need may arise that warrants the group seeking God in prayer. There is nothing wrong with this; the problem is that a steady diet of prayer requests for those outside the group can cause group members to lose interest over time. Keeping it personal helps keep it meaningful for group members.

Encourage group members to go beneath the surface in sharing their prayer requests. God cares about our temporal needs and wants us to bring these to him for his provision. However, he also cares about the deeper work that he wants to do in our lives and wants us to seek him for things like character development and the fruit of the Spirit. The caring, intimate environment of the small group is the perfect place to give and receive prayer for these deeper works in our lives.

> **TIP:** *Focus prayer on God's deeper works in group members' lives by choosing topics for prayer.*

One way to help the group move in this direction is to pick topics for prayer requests. There are many ways to do this; here are a few basic ideas to help you get started:

- Have group members share about a fruit of the Spirit that is particularly lacking in their lives and pray for God to bring that fruit about.

- Read through one of the prayers of Paul for the churches, and have group members single out something from that prayer that they personally need prayer for.

- Pick a topic that you are studying in your Bible study or in church and have members formulate requests around that topic.

The point here is not to discourage prayer for the daily situations and circumstances in people's lives; it is often precisely at those points that group members need to know that the group is pulling for them and praying for them. Rather, the point is to begin to get group members to lift their eyes above the everyday circumstances and discern what God wants to teach them and do in their lives. By getting group members to think in these terms for prayer requests, you will also get them accustomed to viewing their lives more in terms of God's direction for them.

> **TIP:** *Ask good questions to focus the sharing and inform your prayer.*

Finally, ask good questions. Again, balance is needed here to keep from focusing too much on the sharing time. However, a few well-placed questions can actually help focus the sharing time as well as help the group know how to pray. For example, if I receive a request to pray for someone in the hospital, my first question is always, "Is he a Christian?" I ask this question because the answer will determine the focus of my prayer over the situation. Asking good questions can be a way of helping to focus on the deeper spiritual issues underlying the surface of many prayer requests.

Manage the Time

One way to help keep the sharing time from dominating and preventing the group from actually praying is to focus on one person at a time. Have that person share a prayer request, and ask the questions that need to be clarified in order to go to prayer. Then have the group pray over that request until there is a sense that the situation has been covered sufficiently in prayer. Have someone close out that prayer time and then move on to the next person.

I favor this method over having everyone share first and then having everyone pray for several reasons. First, focusing on one person at a time helps group members remember what to pray for. It can be difficult to remember, after six people have talked for twenty to thirty minutes, what the first one wanted prayer for. Second, such a focus promotes agreement in prayer as the group focuses together on one person, rather than skipping around from person to person. This focus will also result in covering each person in the group more thoroughly in prayer. Finally, breaking up the time between sharing and prayer helps keep people involved and concentrating as compared to long periods of sharing and then long periods of prayer (which can lend themselves to people tuning out over time).

If some group members have difficulty expressing their prayer requests succinctly, you may want to consider having everyone write down their requests on an index card (either before coming or during group time). This may help members organize their thoughts. Further, you may want to have group members switch cards before going to prayer, and have each person read the requests on the card they received and then lead the group in prayer for the person who wrote the card.

PRAYER FOR HEALING

One of the most common issues that group members will face and will want prayer for has to do with healing. We often see Jesus and the disciples responding to needs for physical healing in the New Testament, and generally we know that Jesus longs to heal the sick; however, our prayers for the sick need to go beyond just physical healing and relief from symptoms. It's not wrong to pray for these things, but as we do that, we need to be aware that God—for reasons of his own—does not bring such healing in every case, though he could. We are forced to conclude that it is not God's will to heal physically in every case, though it is certainly not wrong for us to ask him to do that.

We have already discussed Paul's prayer for the removal of his thorn in the flesh (2 Cor 12:7-9). This may or may not have involved physical healing, but it is an example of a prayer that God opted to answer in a different way than the pray-er requested. God's greater work in Paul's life was more important than the particular hardship caused by this thorn.

In Luke 4:24-27, Jesus recounts two examples from the Old Testament of God's sovereign choice with regard to providing for physical needs. God sent Elijah to a widow in

Zarephath to provide food for her, when there were many starving widows in Israel. He sent Elisha to cleanse Naaman the Syrian of leprosy, when there were many other unhealed lepers in Israel. We may not understand why God heals one and not another, but it is God's sovereign right to make that choice, and as we pray, we must remember that.

Though we cannot be sure of God's will regarding physical healing in a given situation, we can be sure of some things that God does want to accomplish in circumstances like these. For example, we know that it is God's will to strengthen us through trials (1 Pet 1:6-7), including hardship and discipline (Heb 12:5-12); to develop in us perseverance through trials (Jas 1:2-3; 2 Thess 1:4-5); and to bring honor to Christ as our faith is revealed (1 Pet 1:7).

Consider the story in John 9 about the man born blind whom Jesus healed. We don't know from the story whether or not the man had been praying for healing for years. We don't know whether his parents had been praying. But one thing is clear: according to Jesus, the purpose of his blindness was "that the work of God might be displayed in his life" (Jn 9:3). God had appointed a time for his healing, and that healing had several effects: first, obviously, the man could now see; second, he came to faith in Jesus through the healing; third, Jesus' ministry was confirmed. Even the Pharisees were forced to question among themselves the source of the miracle, confronted as they were with their interpretation of the law on one hand and with Jesus' obvious miraculous power on the other (Jn 9:16). God could have healed this man at any time without waiting for Jesus' earthly ministry; however, he had greater purposes in mind than the physical healing itself.

Another time Jesus healed a paralytic by the pool at Bethesda (Jn 5). This man had been an invalid for thirty-eight years and, though he had often hoped to get into the pool to be healed when the waters were stirred, he was never able to. Why did God choose to wait thirty-eight years to heal this man? We don't know the answer for sure, but John 5:14 might give us a clue. Jesus implies here (as opposed to the blind man of Jn 9) that the man's paralysis had been related in some way to sin in his life. With the healing came conviction of sin also, and Jesus' warning to stop sinning. Perhaps the reason that physical healing did not come to this man sooner was that God saw the deeper need in his life and decided to provide the physical healing in the context of spiritual conviction.

In other instances in the Gospels we see that Jesus' healing often had purposes beyond physical relief: the conviction of sin (Mt 9:2-8), the bringing of faith (Jn 4:46-53), a testimony to the religious leaders of the day (Mt 8:2-4; 12:9-14) and a witness to the multitudes (Mk 5:1-20). As we pray for those in our group who are in need of healing or other material or physical blessings, our prayers should reflect the fact that it is God who is in control, working all things together for our good and for his glory.

Often the most powerful prayers for the sick are those that focus on God's deeper work in the person's life. Such prayers help people to focus on God, to put their faith in him and to see his hand at work in their lives even in the midst of affliction. They take the focus away from the circumstances and put it squarely on God. Often, as a person's focus is shifted away from their own physical condition and on to God, their overwhelming desire becomes to have more of God in their life, with or without physical relief. This was Paul's experience as God told him, in essence, "no relief for you—rely on my grace instead." Indeed, Paul recognized a specific purpose for this weakness—to keep him from becoming conceited. We're left with the impression that, if the thorn was what it took to keep Paul from falling prey to pride, then Paul welcomed it. As we shift our focus from ourselves to God, we're often able to see larger purposes in his working (or apparent nonworking), and often issues of godliness become more important in our lives than physical healing.

Of course, the most famous story of suffering in the Bible is that of Job. Afflicted with loss of possessions, loss of family and loss of health (and further afflicted by the counsel of his so-called friends), confused by the seeming lack of reason behind his suffering, Job expressed uncertainty about the character of God, but he never denied the One whom he knew. And ultimately God did answer Job—not with specific answers to his questions but rather with himself. God has used Job's example of patience and perseverance in the midst of suffering down through the ages as a comfort to those who undergo trials and hardship.

The act of asking for prayer often carries vulnerability with it. Words can be more damaging than usual. And in most cases, the circumstances surrounding suffering are more complex than our limited view into a person's life allows us to understand. When praying for a person's healing (and for other physical and material needs as well—but this is particularly true of healing), unless the person specifically invites counsel, it's best to focus your prayers on lifting the person into God's presence.

Job's friends are the classic biblical example of how not to come alongside someone who is suffering. Rather than simply sitting with Job and praying with him and for him, they felt compelled to offer their "wisdom." Their initial concern for Job (Job 2:12-13) turned into a need to justify themselves (and God) at Job's expense. Sometimes their words were judgmental, accusing Job of sin that resulted in his downfall; sometimes they were theologically correct but altogether unhelpful in their statements about God's wisdom, power and holiness. In reality, God's purposes in allowing Job's suffering were beyond the comprehension of both Job and his companions, as is often the case with us. Speculating on God's intent in situations involving suffering rarely—if ever—produces helpful results.

God sometimes brings needs into the lives of his people specifically for the purpose of displaying his power and compassion in meeting those needs. Sometimes his response is immediate, as in the feeding of the multitudes (Mt 14:13-21; 15:29-38) or the calming of a storm on the sea (Mt 8:23-27). Sometimes he delays in answering prayer but works within hard circumstances until such time as he changes the circumstances. Consider the nation of Israel, enslaved in Egypt for four hundred years. God delayed in bringing them back to the Promised Land because the wickedness of the Amorites, a nation inhabiting that area, had not yet reached its full extreme (Gen 15:16). Although the people of Israel could not possibly have known that this was the reason for God's delay, they could have seen God's work among them in the midst of their oppression by noting how he blessed them and multiplied their numbers even more in the midst of their hardships (Ex 1:12). God was building for himself a nation within Egypt, and he brought them out with a mighty hand in such a way as to spread his fame all the way back to the land of Canaan even before the Israelites reached the area (Josh 2:8-11). In all of this, God had a purpose not only in what he was doing but in the time he took to do it. It's safe to say that God has a much longer view than we do, and his purposes are often beyond our immediate understanding, especially when we are focused on the needs of the moment.

Of course, we are wont to focus on the here and now, and as a result, we often miss God's larger purposes in the midst of our daily lives and particularly in the midst of hardship. It is precisely at this point where group prayer can be so powerful. A small group can surround a person in need with prayer that helps turn the focus to God's larger purposes, lifting the afflicted one's soul and thoughts out of the difficult circumstances and into the presence of God himself. Without preaching to the hurting one (as Job's companions did), it's possible through prayer to bring to bear the depth of God's love and grace even in the midst of affliction. As we do this, we form a cord of three strands that's not easily broken and we help lift up the one who has fallen (Eccles 4:9-12).

As we bring before God the group member who is hurting (whether that hurt be physical, financial, emotional, relational or any other type), we honor God when we pray not only for his specific provision but also for his larger work in that group member's life. One way in which we can help bring this focus about is to ask questions like, "What would you have God do in this situation?" and "Are you open to letting God work in your life in the midst of this situation, in addition to asking him to end it?" As we ask questions like these and as we pray in a context of "Your kingdom come, your will be done," we lift our eyes beyond the immediate situation to the God who is sovereign over every situation.

Two Are Better Than One

Ecclesiastes 4:9-10 says,

> Two are better than one,
> because they have a good return for their work:

> If one falls down,
> his friend can help him up.
> But pity the man who falls
> and has no one to help him up!

A group that supports each other in prayer, lifting up to God the heartfelt requests of group members and praying for God's intervention in each other's lives, is truly helping each other up. Such a group grows stronger as each of its members grows stronger. For many people, their small group is the best place (and perhaps the only place) where they can pray and be prayed for in a way that truly seeks God's best for each other.

Questions for Discussion/Reflection

1. If your group prays for each other, do the requests shared tend to be personal or do they tend to be for people outside the group? What would it take to lead your group into more personal sharing?

111

2. Has your group prayed for physical healing of one of the members? What was the focus of the prayer? How did the group respond?

8

INCORPORATING CONFESSION

JAMES ENCOURAGED BELIEVERS TO "confess your sins to each other and pray for each other so that you may be healed" (Jas 5:16). The area of confession, however, is typically neglected in times of community prayer. And when confession is included, it is typically either silent or very vague. Neither of these is what James had in mind when he penned this verse.

Confession is a particularly difficult area of prayer for individuals, let alone groups. There are many reasons for this. Individually, we often tend to think of ourselves more highly than we ought to. We are so close to our own sinful nature that blind spots develop and we simply do not recognize sin in our own lives. We compare ourselves to some others whom we know, and we see no reason for confession. On the other end of the spectrum, some are so overwhelmed with guilt over their sin that they block it out of their minds. They fear to come before God in confession because they don't want to be reminded of their sinfulness.

Ironically, both of these extremes stem from an incomplete knowledge of God, and failure to know God is perhaps the biggest barrier to praying effectively. The one who fails to see sin in their own life very likely has not come to a full understanding of God's holiness, against which none of us can measure up. Such a person often lacks humility in prayer. The one who is overwhelmed with guilt most likely has not grasped fully God's incredible mercy and grace. This person is incapable of experiencing the depths of God's forgiveness and the resulting freedom to confess and repent.

From a group perspective, confession requires a level of intimacy and openness that, frankly, most groups do not have. Even groups who have met for a period of time often fail to develop the kind of trust required for confession. Many groups have some people who would be comfortable with shared confession and others who would not. People newer to the group will likely be more reluctant to participate in this aspect of prayer.

Finally, shared confession is hard because, in all honesty, most small group leaders struggle (along with everyone else) in this area. Perhaps as you begin this chapter you are wondering if you can really lead your group in this type of prayer. If this is the case, relax. As in other areas in your group, God is not expecting perfection of you before you can lead others. Be willing to learn alongside the group and to grow together in this area. Hopefully this chapter will be of some help.

THE NEED FOR CONFESSION

As with other elements of prayer, the first step toward casting a vision for confession is understanding where your small group is in their own prayer lives with regard to confession. Do your small group members "keep short accounts" with God, confessing their own sin to him regularly? If so, you already have the basis for significant and meaningful shared confession. If not, you may first need to cast a vision in your group for confession in general before moving into vision-casting for shared confession.

A relationship with God begins with confession, repentance and acceptance of Christ's death as the atonement for sin. Recognition and confession of sin and of the need for a Savior begins our walk with God. But confession is not a one-time experience, as though we never sin again after that point. John, in a letter written to believers, writes, "If we claim to be without sin, we deceive ourselves," and again, "if we claim we have not sinned, we make [God] out to be a liar" (1 Jn 1:8, 10). The reality is that we all continue to struggle with sin even as we follow Christ. We're in good company—even Paul struggled continually with sin in his life (Rom 7:14-25).

Far from causing us to despair, however, this ongoing struggle with sin should drive us to God in confession. John, while acknowledging the universality of the struggle with sin, also provides the answer: "If we confess our sins, he is faithful and just and will forgive us our sins and purify us from all unrighteousness" (1 Jn 1:9). We'll come back to this shortly. For now, it is enough to recognize that according to Scripture, sin is a universal condition, requiring confession as the solution. It's safe to say, based on John's instructions, that any small group member who does not believe he or she needs to confess sin is making God out to be a liar.

THE NEED FOR SHARED CONFESSION

All of this is obvious from Scripture. But what about shared confession? Is there a biblical mandate for confession in the presence of other believers? We've already seen James's instruction regarding shared confession. In fact, the Gospels are filled with stories of confession in the presence of others: from Peter's first confession of sinfulness in general upon first meeting Christ (Lk 5:8) to Zacchaeus's confession of cheating people as a tax collector (Lk 19:8) and various other places along the way, public confession was part of meeting and knowing Christ. Paul consistently pointed out sin in the churches to whom he wrote, showing that even those who know Christ and are in fellowship with other believers can fall prey to sin. Jesus himself pointed out sin in five of the seven churches to which he addressed the letters of Revelation 2—3: losing their first love, holding to false teachings, sexual immorality and lukewarm faith. The context of letters written to churches calls for shared confession and communal repentance.

Undoubtedly, shared confession will require some work. Group members must usually be convinced of the value of shared confession. Hearts must be humbled before God, and pride must be put aside. For the group, confidentiality needs to be assured and trust needs to be developed. These developments often take time and require patience for the group and for the leader.

But the benefits brought by shared confession are well worth the work for those groups who successfully incorporate it into their prayer times. Confession (and the accountability that comes with it) provides opportunities to come alongside and encourage the one who struggles. "Two are better than one," Solomon says, "because they have a good return for their work: / If one falls down, / his friend can help him up. / But pity the man who falls / and has no one to help him up!" (Eccles 4:9-10). The group that practices shared confession lifts up the member who has fallen through prayer, encouragement and wise counsel. The group that ignores this important facet of prayer allows its members to struggle on their own with sin.

Shared confession also promotes humility in the group. It's hard to carry on in pride with those who know your faults! Confession allows us to admit our imperfections before God and before others, keeping our hearts soft and humble. This humility in turn promotes unity throughout the group, as group members share openly and honestly, rather than exalting themselves above one another.

Confession also allows for healing. Besides the physical healing mentioned by James, confession paves the way for spiritual healing as God forgives and cleanses, for relational healing as group members are reconciled to each other and to others outside the group, for emotional healing as the loving acceptance of a forgiving God replaces guilt and shame. All of this begins with confession, and much of it will never happen in any other way.

THE THREE Cs: CONFIDENTIALITY, COMPASSION AND COMMITMENT

The first prerequisite for effective shared confession in a group setting is confidentiality. Unless group members can trust that everything said in the group will stay within the group, they will be reluctant to share any areas of struggle or sin. Regardless of the need for shared confession, it will not happen if group members are concerned that struggles brought up in the group might be repeated outside the group. Some groups have gone as far as to sign a covenant which includes a statement about confidentiality. However your group does it, there must be complete trust in the confidentiality of the group for shared confession to become a meaningful part of your life together.

Typically, a group will need to have been together for some time before the members trust each other enough to share their confessions. The introduction of a new person or new people into a group can also set back shared confession for a time; it will take time for the new people to develop the level of trust in the group required for them to participate, and it will take time for the older members of the group to develop trust in the newer members. This is not a warning against inviting new people into your group; just be aware of the dynamics of shared confession and adjust accordingly.

Second, confession must be met with compassion rather than condemnation if it is to be effective in a small group setting. Sin is a universal condition. Even the self-righteous Pharisees and teachers of the law had to drop the stones they had planned to use against a woman caught in adultery when confronted with their own sins (Jn 8:1-11). Interestingly, the only one in the group who could have justly condemned the woman—Jesus—also did not condemn her. Judgment is not given to group members but to God alone. The sin in our own lives ought to make us compassionate toward others when they are confessing sin.

Third, confession absolutely requires commitment to spiritual growth—both on the part of the one confessing sin and on the part of the ones hearing the confession. The group must be committed to prayer and committed to supporting each member if confession is to be real and purposeful. There is no point in confessing sin to a gathering of people who care neither about the sin nor about the one confessing.

Unless the person confessing sin specifically requests it, don't let a time of confession degenerate into a counseling session in your group. Confession seeks not human wisdom but divine forgiveness and cleansing. Whatever similar experiences your group members may have had that they might feel are germane to the situation, no sharing of experience or counseling can replace committed, Christ-centered prayer for the one confessing sin. James is very clear: confession is to be followed by prayer, not by counseling. (In some cases, further steps such as counseling may be needed; however, the small group setting may not provide the best place, or the most experienced counselors, to handle these situations.)

PREPARING THE HEART: PRAISE

One of the best examples in Scripture of confession, forgiveness and cleansing is found in Isaiah 6:1-8, the story of Isaiah's commissioning. The passage begins with Isaiah's vision of God. It isn't until Isaiah sees God as he really is, high and lifted up, majestic and holy, that he recognizes the sin in his own life. As we focus our thoughts on God and see his perfection, we begin to sense our own imperfection.

Opening with a time of praise leads us to focus our hearts on God rather than on ourselves. One of the dangers of confession is that it can be very self-centered—all about me and my sins rather than about the God against whom I've sinned. Such confession is more likely to leave us mired in guilt and shame, whereas confession whose focus is on God leads us to his grace and forgiveness. In confession, as in all aspects of prayer, the goal is to draw nearer to God, not to focus our thoughts on ourselves.

In praise we recognize who God is and what he is like, and this leads us quite naturally into confession. A God who was not holy, for example, could not command our confession. And it would be useless to confess to a God who was not loving and forgiving. We might be able to conceal some sin from a God who was not all-knowing. But since God is all of these things—omniscient, holy, loving, forgiving (along with a host of other qualities), confession is both sensible and beneficial.

ELEMENTS OF CONFESSION

Going back to 1 John 1:9, we can see three elements of confession: the believer confesses sin; God (who is both faithful and just) forgives the sin; God cleanses the believer from unrighteousness. These three elements of confession form a pattern for us to follow in prayer.

Perhaps John had in mind Psalm 51 when he wrote 1 John 1:9. One of the best-known passages on confession in the Bible, this psalm of David shows an application of these three elements. David confesses his sin (Ps 51:3-5), requests God's mercy and forgiveness (Ps 51:1, 9), and pleads for God's cleansing (Ps 51:2, 7, 10-12). See the table "Confession in Two Texts" for a closer examination of the parallels.

Confession in Two Texts: 1 John 1:9 and Psalm 51

Elements	1 John 1:9	Psalm 51
Confession	If we confess our sins	(v. 3) I know my transgressions and my sin is always before me (v. 4) against you, you only, have I sinned and done what is evil in your sight (v. 5) surely I was sinful at birth
God	he is faithful and just	(v. 1) unfailing love; great compassion (v. 4) justified when you judge
Forgiveness	and will forgive us our sins	(v. 1) have mercy on me; blot out my transgressions (v. 9) hide your face from my sins; blot out all my iniquity
Cleansing	and purify us from all unrighteousness	(v. 2) wash away all my iniquity; cleanse me from my sin (v. 7) cleanse me with hyssop; wash me (v. 10) create in me a pure heart; renew a steadfast spirit within me

Psalm 51 is occasioned by Nathan's confrontation of David after his sin of adultery with Bathsheba and the murder of her husband, Uriah. In David's response he recognizes several things about himself with regard to sin. First, he has sinned and needs to be forgiven and cleansed (Ps 51:1-4). Second, this is not the only time he has sinned (note the plural of "transgressions" in Ps 51:1, 3); he's not pretending to be a nearly perfect person who fell just one time. Third, he has a fallen, sinful nature (Ps 51:5). These same three things are true of all of us, and can form the beginning point both of recognizing our need for confession and of actually confessing sin.

The following passages—each of which lists specific categories of behaviors and attitudes that believers are instructed to put behind them—might also be helpful as beginning points for confession.

- Colossians 3:5-9
- Ephesians 5:3-7
- Galatians 5:19-21
- 1 Peter 2:1

STEPS TOWARD SHARED CONFESSION

If your group is not yet ready for shared confession, then there are other ways of incorporating confession into your prayer time. One way is to have a time of silent confession. After opening the prayer time focusing on God and on his attributes, change the topic to confession and allow time for the group to confess their sins silently before God. Though this is not the "ultimate" confession in James's terms, it is a step in the right direction and may help your group members develop confession in their own personal prayer lives.

One particularly poignant exercise we occasionally do at

my church is to hand out black pieces of paper and black ink pens and have people write a particular sin or sins on the piece of paper. (They'll be confidential, since the paper is black!) Each person then takes a hammer and a nail and nails their piece of paper to a wooden cross. Though this again falls a little short of James's command regarding shared confession, it's a great exercise to get the group started down that path. As people picture their sins nailed to the cross, they realize that Jesus has forgiven them, which can free them up to eventually share confessions with one another.

Another step toward shared confession in the group is to have people select partners and confess and pray for each other in pairs. If you have one or two group members who would be comfortable with public confession while the remainder of the group is not, you could arrange with them beforehand to have a time where they will confess their sins before the group and then the group will lay hands on them and pray for their forgiveness and healing. Besides being a great experience for the ones confessing sin, this can provide an example and an encouragement for others in the group to help them move toward public confession.

GOD'S FORGIVENESS AND CLEANSING

We've seen that there are three elements to the confession process: admitting sin, asking for forgiveness and praying for God's cleansing. We've already seen the promise of 1 John 1:9, telling us that God both forgives and cleanses. This forgiveness and cleansing is based not on how "well" we confess, but on God's faithfulness and justice. God is faithful to us, keeping his promise to forgive. And he is a just God, whose legal requirements were satisfied once and for all on the cross.

It's important to end a time of confession with a time of thanksgiving for God's forgiveness and cleansing. This accomplishes several things:

- It focuses the group's thoughts back on God, rather than their own sinfulness.

- It reminds group members to be grateful to God for his blessings.

- It encourages group members to rely on God's forgiveness and move past their sins.

It is in experiencing forgiveness and cleansing that group members are encouraged to consistently bring their sins before the throne of grace. If it helps to get this point across and if your group is at a point of being able to share confession, consider replacing the black paper in the above exercise with white paper; after each person confesses to the group, have that person nail the piece of paper to the cross and have the group pray over that person, thanking God for forgiveness and cleansing.

As group members open themselves up and confess areas of sin and struggle to other group members, this opens the avenues not only to pray for one another in these areas but also to bring accountability and even personal help to these situations. Again, there needs to be a certain level of trust and intimacy (not to mention a commitment to spiritual growth) among group members in order for this to happen, but if these are present, then the discipline of confessing sin to each other and praying for each other can be a significant step in growing the group closer to God.

If spiritual growth is an objective of your group, confession and accountability need to be part of your group's shared experience. Following the guidelines in this chapter can help you lead your group into a meaningful practice of shared confession that can provide God another avenue for bringing about growth and maturity in your group members.

QUESTIONS FOR DISCUSSION/REFLECTION

1. Does your group currently participate in shared confession in any way? If not, how open do you think group members would be to the idea?

2. How does your group rate with respect to the "three Cs": confidentiality, compassion and commitment? If any of these is a problem in your group, what can you do to grow the group in that area?

3. If your group is not yet quite ready for groupwide shared confession, what steps do you think you could take in that direction?

STRETCHING YOUR GROUP'S PRAYER MUSCLES

THERE IS NO MAGIC FORMULA for prayer. Prayer, as an expression of our relationship with a living God, is by nature a growing part of our lives. This chapter is meant not to provide formulas for how to run your small group's prayer time, but rather to give some ideas to help you stretch your small group a bit in prayer. These ideas build on the principles and practices we have already discussed.

PRAISE AND THANKSGIVING

One of the most difficult things for a group to do in prayer is to spend time praising and thanking God without asking for further blessings. "Father, thank you for the funds you have provided for our church; please continue to provide the resources needed for our building program." The prayer starts off with thanksgiving and ends with a petition that God will continue what he has already been doing. Of course, there is nothing wrong with such combination prayers; however, it can be a very stretching exercise to try to get your group to focus solely on praise and thanksgiving without any petition for a time.

We tend to spend most of our prayer time (as individuals and as groups) in petition—whether for ourselves or for others. Praise and thanksgiving are not a "higher" form of prayer than petition, but our groups can be a bit "praise challenged" in our prayer lives. A time of praise and thanksgiving at the beginning of the prayer time—with no petition—can really help the group to focus on the God to whom we bring our needs.

If you choose to try an exercise like this, be patient with your group. Generally, people are not accustomed to offering praise and thanksgiving to God outside the context of bringing needs to him. Group members are going to "slip up" occasionally and sneak a request into their praise time. Give very clear instructions at the beginning of your prayer time about how the time will be divided up. Let your group know that you will shift the focus when it is time to move from praise and thanksgiving to petition; that way, they know where the "boundaries" are. And when that inevitable "slip up" occurs, simply follow up with a brief prayer that includes only praise or thanksgiving to help your group get back on track. With practice, group members will become more comfortable with a time of praise and thanksgiving.

The common distinction between praise and thanksgiving is that praise focuses on God's attributes (holiness, mercy, etc.) while thanksgiving focuses on what he has done (giving us salvation, providing for our needs, etc.). This is a purely artificial distinction; a study of Psalms will reveal that the psalmists tend to use the terms interchangeably. Nonetheless, these definitions can be helpful in giving us two distinct ways of focusing our thoughts on God. In praise, we focus on God's nature; in thanksgiving, we focus on his intervention in our lives and the lives of others.

AGREEING IN PRAYER

We have already looked at Jesus' promise in Matthew 18:19 regarding God answering prayer where two or more believers are in agreement. And we have discussed the idea of the group silently agreeing in prayer while an individual prays aloud. Here are a couple of ideas for making that agreement explicit.

First, have your group say a collective "Amen" after each person prays. This practice can break up the flow of the prayer meeting a bit, but it does help each person focus on what is being prayed rather than thinking about what they are going to pray later. It's one way to get the group to "agree in prayer."

Another exercise would be to have one person agree aloud in prayer with the person who has just prayed by restating the prayer. Obviously, this is difficult to do with long prayers, but if prayers are focused and brief, this practice can help build agreement in the group and keep the prayer time from jumping around too much.

If your group is having difficulty with brevity in your prayer times, here's another exercise you might try. For an entire prayer meeting, have people pray in prayers of one sentence only (no fair adding multiple dependent phrases and clauses!!).

This is a very stretching exercise and will be quite difficult for most people at first, but there is no better way to focus prayer.

One way to practice this would be for a designated leader to open prayer for a given topic (with just one sentence, of course!) and then have the rest of the group follow with one-sentence prayers related to that topic. When the leader senses that the topic has been fully covered in prayer, he or she moves on to the next one.

This can also be a great exercise for building up agreement in prayer, as group members are forced to stay mentally with the person praying and keep the focus to one topic at a time. If you try this, be sure to encourage group members to pray multiple times on the same topic if they feel so led. This will help ensure that people don't feel compelled to pray longer prayers to make sure everything gets covered.

Sentence prayers can lead to a fairly "choppy" feel to the prayer time, so you probably won't want to pray this way over a long period of time. But if your group has a problem with brevity, this is a great way to start developing the discipline of praying simply and succinctly.

Prayers from Scripture

Sometimes using the model of prayers from Scripture can help group members both express themselves and grow deeper in their prayer lives. The Psalms, for example, include many prayers of confession, thanksgiving and praise, and petition. You could focus a prayer time on a particular psalm that seems to have relevance to the group; read through the psalm and discuss it a bit, then go to prayer with everyone understanding the meaning and attitude behind the psalm.

Paul's prayers for the churches (see, for example, Phil 1:3-11; Eph 1:15-23; Col 1:3-14) are great models of intercession. As you focus on these prayers, you will see that they are concerned with issues of spiritual life and growth and with living godly lives. These prayers can be an antidote to constant praying about temporal circumstances.

PRAYERS THAT REACH BEYOND THE GROUP

Another way to stretch your group's "prayer muscles" is to grow your group in seeing prayer as part of the mission of the group—that is, as a way in which the group can reach beyond themselves. Prayer along these lines can really unite a group and can help to lift the group's eyes to other needs.

There are many ways in which you could do this, and a list of resources to help you is provided in appendix B. Here are just a few possibilities:

- prayer for your church
- prayer for local/national/world leaders
- prayer for a specific country (or countries)
- prayer for missionaries (especially missionaries known by someone in the group or sent out by your church)
- prayer for global issues such as poverty, war, famine, etc.
- prayer for people who have not yet heard the gospel around the world
- prayer for the persecuted church around the world
- prayer for specific ministries in your area

Group members in general will tend to be passionate about different things. Encourage them to develop areas of passion in prayer and even to lead the group in prayer around those areas. For example, if a group member is passionate about evangelism, let him lead a time of prayer for the lost. If someone else is concerned about the persecuted church, let her lead a time of prayer around that topic. In this way, you'll keep your prayer times fresh, encourage the contributions of group members and inspire group members to pray about different topics.

These ideas are meant as suggestions for keeping your group growing in prayer. Once your group has mastered the basics of praying together, you may find some of these helpful to keep your community prayer life from becoming stagnant. The key here is to make sure that your community prayer life remains dynamic, exciting and powerful. Don't let it stagnate or become deprioritized. Mix up how you pray together to keep it interesting. Challenge group members continually to take a next step in praying, both together and individually. As your group grows in prayer, so will the ways in which God works in your group.

Prayer Controversies

Community prayer should be a great unifying factor in your small group. Praying for each other, focusing attention on God's intervention and work in group members' lives, can be one of the most encouraging and uplifting experiences in the Christian life. As you learn to pray together more effectively as a group, the experience of unity will continue to heighten.

This pleases Jesus, who prayed for unity among the believers (Jn 17). However, even a practice as unifying as community prayer can become divisive if "prayer controversies" are not dealt with effectively. Let's look at a few prayer "hot buttons"—types of prayer that most commonly divide groups and prevent true agreement and unity in prayer. Then we'll draw some conclusions from those areas and outline some general principles to help guide our prayer time in the context of bringing unity in prayer out of a diversity of backgrounds, beliefs and experiences.

Praying in tongues. It is not the intent of this book to espouse a doctrine regarding praying in tongues. Scripture speaks to this practice, but exactly what Scripture says is interpreted differently by different people. Still, it would be irresponsible not to address the topic in a book about praying in a small group setting.

As with the topic of group prayer in general, Scripture is pretty much silent as far as giving specific instructions on the topic of praying in tongues. Although Paul mentions praying in tongues a couple of times, the only actual instructions he gives regarding tongues are in a different setting than prayer—that of a prophetic utterance given by God in a tongue (1 Cor 14:26-28, 39). Extensive doctrines both for and against praying in tongues have been developed from very little actual scriptural instruction.

If you are in a group whose custom is to pray in tongues and if group members are comfortable with that doctrinally and in practice, then there is no reason from a community prayer standpoint why you should not continue to do so. My only caution would be that the aspect of prayer represented by praying in tongues is only one of many aspects of prayer, and other aspects such as confession, intercession and petition should not be neglected. There should be balance in the way that your group approaches prayer. My own limited experience indicates that such balance is often lacking in groups where praying in tongues is a normal part of the prayer experience.

If, on the other hand, one or more members of your group are not accustomed to praying in tongues and are not comfortable with the practice, then Paul's teachings about acting in love toward your brothers and sisters in the faith should take precedence (see 1 Cor 10:23—11:1). Paul's example in this passage was a significant issue in his day—that of eating meat sacrificed to idols. Paul explained that since an idol has no real significance, the fact that meat has been offered to an idol really has no meaning when it comes to eating or not eating. However, when in the presence of a person for whom eating such meat would be a problem, Paul urges the believers to abstain in deference to that person's conscience (1 Cor 10:28-29). The principle here is that of not causing another Christian to stumble, for that would pervert the freedom that God gives. Rather, acting out of love for a Christian with different beliefs, the believer is to restrict his or her own freedom.

As applied to praying in tongues, the principle would be this: If you are in a group with people who do not practice praying in tongues, then you also should abstain unless you have specifically talked about it and agreed about it beforehand. While it may be permissible for you to pray in tongues, it is not beneficial in this setting (1 Cor 10:23). To insist on your own way and pray in tongues despite the possible discomfort to others is to act not in love but in selfishness. It is no coincidence that Paul starts his great treatise on love in 1 Corinthians 13 with these words: "If I speak in the tongues of men and of angels, but have not love, I am only a resounding gong or a clanging cymbal." If you insist on praying in tongues despite the discomfort or inexperience of others in the group, then you are not acting in love toward them.

Most groups, of course, have some level of understanding—either implicit or explicit—about whether praying in tongues is part of their prayer experience together. These thoughts apply especially to groups formed from churches of different doctrines, perhaps in a community prayer gathering or other such setting. If you are in such a setting and your practice is to pray in tongues, then the principle of acting in love would dictate that you discuss the matter with any in the group whom you do not know before going to prayer. If there is not unanimous agreement on the practice, then it is inappropriate in that setting.

"Spiritual warfare" prayer. Most people who have been praying for some time and who have studied much about prayer have been introduced to the concept of prayer as spiritual warfare. The New Testament makes many references to this concept that prayer is a means of fighting the unseen spiritual war whose results we see in the surface "battles" around us. However, as with praying in tongues, entire prayer theologies are sometimes developed around a couple of oblique references and key terms. The accuracy of these beliefs and practices is not provable, because most of the biblical references in this area are highly symbolic and are not explained. More important to the concept of community prayer, interpretations of these ideas vary widely and most of them are not known to people relatively new to the area of prayer. This can make prayer that is explicitly along

the lines of spiritual warfare actually divisive in a group and counterproductive to community prayer.

Paul says in 2 Corinthians 10:4, "The weapons we fight with are not the weapons of the world. On the contrary, they have divine power to demolish strongholds." He expands on this idea in the famous "armor of God" passage in Ephesians 6: "Our struggle is not against flesh and blood, but against the rulers, against the authorities, against the powers of this dark world and against the spiritual forces of evil in the heavenly realms" (Eph 6:12). Paul goes on to list several metaphorical pieces of "armor" that the Christian should be careful to put on for this spiritual warfare, and ends the passage with an emphasis on prayer: "Pray in the Spirit on all occasions with all kinds of prayers and requests" (Eph 6:18).

But what is a spiritual "stronghold"? What are its characteristics, and how would we demolish it? What does it mean to pray "in the Spirit"? Does this have reference to praying in tongues (an idea unsupported by the immediate context)? Or is it referring to something else? Is praying in the Spirit the same thing as praying in Jesus' name? What would it really look like to put on the metaphorical armor of God?

The point here is not to try to develop a theology of spiritual warfare prayer. There are probably as many answers to these questions as there are readers of this book. And that's the point. Your group members—if they have even been exposed to this concept at all—are likely to have different ideas and interpretations about what these passages mean and how they should be applied in prayer. You may have some group members who are completely unfamiliar with these concepts and will be intimidated by prayer along these lines, along with "seasoned prayer warriors" whose prayer lives are dominated by spiritual warfare. Next to praying in tongues, spiritual warfare prayer can be one of the most divisive concepts facing a group trying to pray together.

So, how do you handle this? Some of the principles here are similar to those for praying in tongues. First, if your whole group is not comfortable with spiritual warfare prayer, then it is best left for the prayer closet for the time being. One thing you can do as a group is to study the concept of spiritual warfare together and begin to introduce that kind of prayer to your group prayer time. If you decide to study this topic, be aware of one thing: It's easy to "go off the deep end" on this topic, and you will need to carefully select the type of study you will do in order to avoid this.

For example, in Matthew 16:19, Jesus says, "I will give you [Peter, cf. Mt 16:18] the keys of the kingdom of heaven; whatever you bind on earth will be bound in heaven, and whatever you loose on earth will be loosed in heaven." Similarly, in Matthew 18:18 Jesus says, "I tell you [the disciples, cf. Mt 18:1] the truth, whatever you bind on earth will be bound in heaven, and whatever you loose on earth will be loosed in heaven." What does Jesus mean by "binding" and "loosing"? He does not explain it. Was this a promise given to Peter and to the disciples only, or was it meant for all Christians down through the ages? We don't know; these are the *only* two places in the New Testament where this kind of language is used.

Still, with this small a foundation, whole practices of "binding and loosing" have developed in prayer. To some people, it's important to use the actual words *bind* and *loose;* to others, the language is less important than the concept.

Usually the terms are used in the context of "binding" Satan or demons and "loosing" angels or the Holy Spirit. These may very well be correct applications of Jesus' commands (assuming they were meant for all Christians), but because there is so little Scripture in support of this practice, different people will practice it in very different ways. Some assume the authority themselves as Jesus originally gave it to the disciples: "I bind the power of Satan." Others see the need for Satan to be bound but defer to God to do that: "Please bind the power of Satan." Is one more correct than the other? Scripture does not say.

If your group is going to practice spiritual warfare prayer (and there is certainly good reason why you should do this), then you should come to some kind of agreement on what your role as a group in spiritual warfare is, and how you will agree in prayer on this. Not everyone needs to believe the exact same things about spiritual warfare, but when you pray as a group, it's key to get agreement on how you are praying. This is especially true if your group has one or more new members in it. More than one believer, unacquainted with the language of spiritual warfare, has wondered if the group is really a cult, so unfamiliar are the concepts and terms they're using.

One final note about spiritual warfare prayer: This sort of prayer gets Satan's attention. The enemy may not be too concerned about the one who prays for physical healing, financial blessing or any number of other topics. But the ones who intentionally engage in spiritual warfare through prayer will most certainly disturb him and will often find themselves the object of his attacks. It would be unfair to your group members to allow this kind of prayer without first discussing the possible ramifications and getting agreement to press ahead.

Prayer and the gift of healing. Again, it's not the purpose of this book to espouse a doctrine of the spiritual gift of healing, but since that gift is often employed in a context of prayer (and even community prayer), it seems appropriate to address the topic briefly in terms of community prayer.

As far as I can tell, there is every reason to believe that the gift of healing is alive and well in the church today. This does not mean that everything that is called the "gift of healing" really is the spiritual gift, and it doesn't mean that the gift is always used correctly. Many public demonstrations of the "gift of healing" tend to glorify the one using the gift, rather than the One who gave it. We can say with confidence that this is not a proper use of the gift of healing, if the real gift is even in evidence.

However, the fact that a gift can be misused does not mean that it cannot be used correctly. There is no reason to suppose that James's command to "pray for each other so that you may be healed" (Jas 5:16) has been rescinded, and no good reason that I can see to believe that the spiritual gift of healing has ceased to be in use in the church.

In a context of community prayer, however, healing prayer may tend toward the same divisive effect as praying in tongues or spiritual warfare prayer. Most likely, group members will come to the idea of the gift of healing with different backgrounds and different beliefs about how (and if) the gift should be used. It's important, therefore, if your group is going to practice this kind of prayer, to make sure that there is a common understanding of the gift of healing as a basis.

Note that I am not talking about our rather common prayers for someone to be healed of an illness or an injury. Here, I am discussing the spiritual gift of healing, which is different from simply interceding for the sick or injured. A case could be made that all of us should be praying for the sick; however, the Holy Spirit has given the gift of healing to those whom he has specifically chosen. In the exercise of this gift, then, it's important to have a common basis of understanding in your group. For example, if your group is going to practice the gift of healing in a context of community prayer, it will be divisive if half the group doesn't even believe that the gift is still extant in the church.

Following, then, are a couple of things that the group should understand before looking to practice this gift. First, group members need to have a common belief about whether or not the spiritual gift of healing is still active in the church today. Many Christians believe that the so-called sign gifts (of which healing is one) are no longer valid in the church. Others believe that these gifts are still valid and active. Your group members need to be of the same mind on this as a basis for using the gift. If that's not the case, then the gift (if it exists in your group) would best be used in a more private setting than the small group context. Additionally, if this is an ongoing issue in your group, you should consider doing a Bible study together about spiritual gifts in general or the gift of healing in particular to try to come to a common understanding. Again, choose your study carefully if you are going to do this. If your church has a doctrine regarding spiritual gifts or the specific gift of healing (and if your small group is a church-based small group), then that might be a good place to start.

Second, if you are going to practice the gift of healing, then obviously you need someone in the group who has that gift. Methods for determining spiritual gifts differ, and it's not an exact science, but there should be some objective confirmation (as far as that's possible) that a person in your group has this gift before you attempt to use it; otherwise, you could end up doing more damage than good. Again, a study on spiritual gifts or a spiritual gifts test could come in useful here. Confirmation from church leaders would also be good evidence.

Finally, make sure that God is the one being glorified and that the gift is being exercised in a fitting and appropriate way.

Praying in Love

Tongues, spiritual warfare prayer and the gift of healing are only a few of many areas of prayer that carry with them some controversy. The principle of showing love to all the members of the group requires us to practice the "lowest common denominator" in these areas. If there are people in the group who are not comfortable with a particular prayer practice, then that practice should be left for the prayer closet.

Be careful that no air of superiority develops among the more "aggressive" pray-ers in the group. Paul in 1 Corinthians 10 does not imply that it's the more spiritually mature people who can eat meat sacrificed to idols, or that it is the less mature believers who feel restricted because of conscience. (A similar passage in Romans 14 does refer to the believer whose "faith is weak" and who eats only vegetables. The fact that Paul does not repeat the "weak faith" idea in 1 Corinthians likely indicates that the situation was specific to the Roman church. Some of the most spiritually mature people I know happen to be vegetarians!) Believing differently on matters like this is not an indication of spiritual maturity or lack of it, but behaving in an unloving way toward brothers and sisters in the group is definite evidence of a lack of spiritual maturity.

As your group grows in prayer, you need to be very much on your guard against possible divisions over issues like this. Satan does not want your group to pray together. There are many things you could do that won't bother him a bit, but praying together is not one of them. He will do whatever he can to keep your group from praying together. It's a matter of irony that he will even use Scripture about prayer to bring division if he can (just like he used Scripture to tempt Jesus). If this seems to be becoming a problem in your group, don't neglect it. Earnestly pray to God about it, and if necessary, talk to the people who are causing the division (as you would about any other issue in your group causing division). But don't stop praying; that's exactly the victory that Satan wants.

Similarly, as we've seen before, certain prayer topics can be sources of division in your group. Be sensitive to these areas and aware of whether people are praying God's agenda or their own. Teach your group to pray God's agenda, and leave areas where personal agendas get in the way for the prayer closet.

The admonitions in this chapter are not meant to keep a group from experiencing diversity in prayer. Rather, they are meant to help you recognize and prepare for issues that could potentially be divisive in a community prayer setting. Diverse prayer styles are not in and of themselves detractors from the environment of community prayer; in fact, group members can often learn from each other's prayer styles and prayer strengths.

Just as God has gifted each of the members of the body of Christ differently, so also he has wired us a little differently in terms of how we pray (both in style and in focus). Recognizing this, not everyone in the group needs to be forced into the same prayer mold. Rather, help the group mold diverse prayer styles into a community prayer environment that promotes agreement in prayer and focus on Christ. The practices of community prayer discussed in this book should help create this type of prayer environment.

QUESTIONS FOR DISCUSSION/REFLECTION

1. Does anyone in your group have a particular prayer passion? How could you incorporate that into the group's prayer time?

2. Are there types of prayer in your group that tend to divide the group or cause some people not to participate? How will you deal with those issues to bring about greater unity in prayer in your group?

OTHER PRAYER CONTEXTS

THIS IS A BOOK ABOUT COMMUNITY PRAYER, the ideal prayer context in a small group setting. Therefore, we purposely have not discussed in detail other prayer contexts, such as private prayer (which I have often referred to as "the prayer closet"), corporate prayer or one-on-one intercessory prayer. It is beyond the scope of this book to go into detail about these prayer settings and all that they imply. However, there are some principles from community prayer that can also enhance prayer in these other settings. Those principles and applications are the focus of this chapter.

THE PRAYER CLOSET
Throughout this book, we have often differentiated between the prayer closet and the community prayer setting. We started off by noting that private prayer involves a one-dimensional relationship (vertical), while community prayer adds a second (horizontal) dimension. Several times in dis-

cussing various practices of community prayer, we have made a statement along the lines of "this is okay for private prayer, but not ideal for community prayer."

In private prayer, we don't face issues such as the need to promote agreement in prayer, the problem of praying too long so that others are not able to track with the prayer or (for the most part) the tendency to address group members in prayer. In private prayer, God wants us to pour out our hearts to him in worship, praise, intercession, petition, confession and so on. Issues of community prayer like length, wording and topical focus don't present problems in private prayer.

Still, there are some principles of community prayer that, when applied to the prayer closet, can enhance our private prayer lives. We'll focus briefly on a few of those in this chapter, keeping in mind that some of the "wrongs" of community prayer are merely matters of preference in private prayer.

Brevity and focus. Remember the quote from Brother Lawrence? "It isn't necessary to be too verbose in prayer, because lengthy prayers encourage wandering thoughts." This was a comment about private prayer, and if it was true in Brother Lawrence's day, how much more is it true in our day of ultra-short attention spans! My intent here is not to discourage long prayer times but rather to suggest that prayers about individual topics be kept brief and focused. What is true here in community prayer is also true in private prayer—God does not need much detail about the situations for which we're praying or the people for whom we're interceding. He already knows more about our prayer subjects than we do! If you've ever felt overburdened by the number of situations for which you are praying, perhaps some of that can be overcome by praying more simply and directly. It isn't the number of words in our prayers that moves God to act but the heart behind those prayers.

Although you're not in danger of addressing people rather than God in a private prayer setting, there can still be a temptation to leave God out of the equation in prayer. When our prayers are worded in terms of asking that situations would change or that people would act, rather than directly asking God to be the change agent, we're focusing more on the circumstances than we are on God. Do we truly understand that the only way that hearts will change is if God changes them? Do we really believe that the only way our world will improve is if God improves it? Or do we pray as though these things could happen on their own?

You'll probably find that as you concentrate on addressing God in community prayer it will also become a habit in your private prayer life. Not surprisingly, cultivating the practice of addressing prayer directly to God in the prayer closet will also positively impact your community prayer life.

The same is true of our focus in prayer. When we focus on the circumstances and people for whom we pray, not only do our prayers tend to become unnecessarily long, but also our faith can be tested and even weakened. When we focus instead on the God to whom we pray, our faith is strengthened as our eyes are lifted to him.

Thy will be done. Submitting our prayers to God's will is also a great practice for the prayer closet. As we submit to his will, we are praying in tune with the prayer Jesus taught and practicing his command to seek first God's kingdom (Mt 6:33). This does not mean that we keep our deepest desires and needs hidden from God, but rather that we bring them before him, expressing our hearts and then entrusting the outcome to his perfect will. Jesus himself provided the model for praying this way in Gethsemane. Everything that is true about praying God's will in the community prayer context is still true in the prayer closet.

The same is true for praying "kingdom prayers" in the midst of our circumstances. Emphasizing in our private prayer lives the kinds of things that Paul prayed for the churches puts in context our prayers about more temporal things. We pray for temporal blessings, yes; but we pray for them in light of eternity and with our eyes and hearts fixed on things above, not on earthly things. We pray for them in a context not of earthly, selfish motivations but rather in a context of wanting God's name to be honored in our lives and in the lives of those around us.

ONE-ON-ONE INTERCESSION

There is a "middle ground" between community prayer and private prayer: one-on-one intercession. As with other prayer contexts, this one has several variations; what is appropriate in one setting may or may not be appropriate in another. By one-on-one intercession, I mean a situation in which someone comes to you for prayer and you pray together over the person's need. This happens in many different settings. At my church, for example, we have "elder prayer" once a month after our midweek service. Anyone in the congregation who wishes someone to pray with them personally is invited to come, and a group of trained prayer leaders is present to pray with those who come. In a similar setting, we also hold several leadership conferences each year at our church, and we have a prayer team available to pray with any conference attendee who has a particular need for prayer.

Obviously, this is a very different setting from the one in which a close friend pours out his or her heart to you in your living room and you go to prayer together. In a setting like that, the nature of your relationship and the experiences you've had together (especially in prayer) will most likely dictate how you pray. Although there is some value in applying some of the principles we've talked about in this book to such a setting, here we will explore community prayer concepts in a context of intercessory prayer for someone you don't know.

Though of course situations will differ and may call for variations in exactly how you pray, I'd suggest the following three general steps for one-on-one intercession, each of which I'll explain shortly:

1. Listen "in the Spirit."

2. Prepare to pray.

3. Pray.

These steps seem so simple and obvious as not to need mentioning, but I list them for two reasons: First, to emphasize that the purpose of your time together is to get to step 3; and second, to point out that there is a need to briefly set the ground rules for how you will pray together. Let's look at each step more closely.

Listen "in the Spirit." First, as an intercessor, you must keep in mind that your primary role in the time you have is not to act as counselor, adviser or teacher. You are there to pray; nothing you can do together will be more significant or have a greater effect on the situation than imploring the intervention of an all-powerful, all-loving God. If the person has further needs (e.g., for counseling or resources), the most effective way to meet those is to engage someone else in the process (after you have prayed, of course) who is equipped to meet those needs. At our church, we have a "lay pastors" ministry composed of volunteers who have been trained in areas such as counseling and are available during our intercessory prayer times should they be needed. Of course, if you are equipped to meet those needs yourself and if the setting is appropriate, you are free to do that; just be sure that you draw a boundary around the prayer time and make that a real focus.

Listening to the situation is very closely related to the sharing of prayer requests that we discussed in the community prayer context, and the same principles apply. Listen actively and focus the conversation on details relevant to the prayer need. If you get someone who starts giving you an autobiographical sketch, you may need to rein that in and help the person to focus more narrowly on the situation for which prayer is being requested. You may also need to ask some questions for clarification in order to help you pray. If you get someone who comes asking for prayer for a sick friend or relative in the hospital, one of the first things that should come to your mind (and one of the first questions out of your mouth) should be whether or not the person is a Christian, because the answer to that question should definitely affect the way you pray for the person.

Let the Holy Spirit guide what you are hearing. Ask him for discernment, and be open to "hearing" unexpressed needs that may be below the surface of the prayer needs that the person is bringing. As an example, recall the situation in Matthew 9 in which Jesus healed a paralytic. Jesus recognized instantly that there were two levels of need for him to address: the surface need for physical healing and the deeper spiritual need for forgiveness of sins. Jesus met both of these needs. So as we listen to the one sharing needs for prayer, we should be tuned in to not only the expressed needs (which will more often than not be on a surface level) but also the deeper spiritual needs (of which the person may not even be aware). I know that this can seem like a daunting task, but remember that it is the Holy Spirit who teaches us how to pray and who intercedes on our behalf.

Prepare to pray. It may not seem intuitive that you need to do this, but you should realize that many people who come for intercessory prayer are probably a bit uncertain about what to expect. Unless you've prayed with the person previously, they are probably unfamiliar with your prayer style or with the logistics of how the process works. As is the case in community prayer, it's usually a good idea to establish the "ground rules" before going to prayer—both to set the person at ease regarding expectations and to guide your time productively in prayer.

First, if there is something that you feel a need to say to the person, by all means say it before going to prayer. Actually, this is a particular weakness of mine. There are occasions in which I have a sense that a person really has God's heart for an issue, and I want to affirm that in the person. I often do this in the prayer time itself, couched in terms of thanking God for that person's heart. It's not wrong to be thankful in prayer for God's work in bringing a person's heart close to his own, but if I want to affirm the person, I should do so before we actually pray, as that addresses the person and not God.

Similarly, if you sense that a person is in need of encouragement or a reminder of some attribute of God (love, sovereignty, etc.), find a way to express that to the person before going to prayer. The idea here is to avoid preaching to the person while praying and to focus the prayer time itself on addressing God, as we've discussed previously. A brief word of encouragement to the person for whom you are praying can help you keep the prayer time itself focused on God. We'll look at an example of this shortly.

Moreover, if you do sense the need to address the person briefly, avoid getting carried away; remember, the goal of your time together is to pray—and, in prayer, to focus on addressing God. What's true of community prayer is also true of one-on-one intercession: God should be the one being addressed.

Finally, make sure that the person knows exactly how the prayer time is going to work. I find it most effective to ask the person if they want to pray also or if they just want me to pray. I don't try to push one way or the other on this; I simply want to know what the person's expectations are. Some people who come for prayer would be mortified to think that they are expected to pray out loud with a stranger; some who come are very comfortable praying with others and want to participate. It takes about fifteen seconds to ask and receive the answer to this question.

If the person wants to participate in prayer out loud, then you need to establish exactly how you will do that. Do you expect to go back and forth many times? How will you both know when you're done praying? Part of the answer to this question will depend on the exact setting. Has only one person come for prayer and do you have a significant amount of time to spend? Or are you in a situation in which you will be expected to pray for several people (one at a time) and need to limit the amount of time you spend with each one? If you're in a limited-time situation, I suggest that you set things up so that you will open in prayer, then the other person will pray, and then you'll close. This way, you both know when you are done, and the time factor can be more manageable.

If you find it helpful, you may also want to mention a quick word about the fact that God already knows the needs you are about to express to him in prayer. This can be a way of preventing a person from going into a lot of unnecessary detail in prayer and can help keep the focus on God rather than on the circumstances. Again, what's true of community prayer is also true here: God does not need the details, and the more details you or the other person provide in prayer, the more likely the thoughts are to wander, preventing true agreement in prayer.

Pray. Pray simply, briefly and directly. You may be surprised to learn this, but most people who come for prayer do not require you to pray long, in-depth, flowery prayers. In the back of their minds, that may be part of their expectations (because they don't know that prayer doesn't have to be that way), but you will exceed their expectations by praying God-focused, simple and direct prayers.

As you pray, be sure to keep your focus on God and not on the circumstances about which you are praying. The principle of praying "kingdom prayers" also applies here. If you have listened in the Spirit and if God has revealed to you some deeper needs, be sure to focus on those deeper spiritual issues in prayer. If you sense that God wants to do a particular work in a person's life, pray specifically for that work. Avoid stating in prayer, however, what you believe to be the work that God wants to do. Such "prayer" usually leaves a person feeling preached to (an accurate feeling). We know, for example, that God uses trials to produce in us perseverance (Jas 1:2-3). This does not necessarily mean that the production of perseverance is the purpose of the trial, of course; it may be or it may not be. But perseverance can still be produced, even if that's not the reason for the trial. Yet even if you believe that God is using trials in a person's life to bring about perseverance, don't pray, "Lord, we know that you use trials in our lives to develop in us perseverance." God already knew that and didn't need to be reminded. The person for whom you're praying might need to hear it, but if they do, say it to them directly; don't couch it in prayer.

Here's an example of a "sermonizing" prayer that needs to be avoided: "Lord, we know that you bring trials into our lives to develop patience and perseverance in us. We need this perseverance in order to come to full maturity. We trust that you are allowing this trial to bring this perseverance and maturity to so-and-so, and we look forward to seeing how you will work in his life." A prayer like this, full of scriptural truth, is not really a prayer at all but a bit of a mini-sermon directed to the one with whom you are praying.

Instead of sermonizing to the person for whom you should be interceding, address the person if you need to and set up how you will pray. "God often permits trials in our lives to bring about perseverance and maturity. So I'm going to pray for God to bring an end to your trial [healing, job, whatever] and I'm also going to pray that he will work in your life during whatever time he chooses to let this trial continue." Then address God in prayer: "Father, we pray tonight that you will somehow use this trial to bring so-and-so closer to you. Strengthen his faith and grow him in perseverance and maturity. And Lord, in accordance with your will, please bring healing to him in your timing."

There is a world of difference between the above two scenarios. In the first, you have asked nothing of God. Instead, you have preached to the one for whom you're supposed to be interceding. Although they might not have been able to identify it exactly as preaching, they can sense on some level that what has really happened here is that you have focused on teaching them a lesson—a lesson they may well need to learn, but one that's not likely to be received well in place of true intercessory prayer.

In the second scenario, you have shared the same basic information with the person, but you have done it in a way that sets up how you will pray. Most likely the person will react positively to this because you have couched it not in terms of sermonizing but in terms of explaining how you are about to pray. You've avoided preaching; you've spent your time in intercession; and you've also modeled for the person how they can pray on their own regarding this situation on an ongoing basis. You have prayed and you have empowered them to pray. Modeling prayer like this is a much more effective tool for encouraging ongoing life-change than teaching someone how they should believe (or even how they should pray). By helping them to see God working in their life even in the midst of trial, you've focused their thoughts on kingdom issues rather than strictly on the earthly situation. Although this may have also been your intent with the prayer in the first scenario, the second prayer much more effectively accomplishes this.

A variation. You may occasionally encounter a situation in intercession in which several people come to you wanting to join the prayer for one individual. I've had situations in our elder prayer where an entire small group has come to pray for an individual in that group who was facing a specific trial. These situations can be sweet times of community prayer, or they can be a bit of a mess.

In a case like this, since you have several people present, treat it as a small group prayer time (which is really what it is; you are simply being asked to lead the time). Go through the same steps as above regarding listening and preparing for prayer. The group is implicitly looking to you to lead the time, so set it up clearly and explain how you will pray. You may not have as much back-and-forth (in terms of question and answer) with the individual in this setting, but suggest a couple of ideas for prayer that involve not only the direct situation but also kingdom prayers surrounding that situation. Ask the group to pray briefly and simply and encourage them to pray more than once if God so leads them. Let the group know that you will close the prayer time when you sense that they are done. As you open the time in prayer, be sure to ask God to reveal to the group how he would have them pray in this situation.

When someone comes to you for intercession, realize that that's exactly what they want and need—intercession, not counseling, teaching, exhortation or anything else. Focus your time and energy on intercession. If there are further needs, see if someone trained in those areas might be able to help with them.

CORPORATE PRAYER

By "corporate prayer" I mean a situation in which one person stands in front of a larger group and prays on their behalf. Some community prayer concepts can make corporate prayer more effective. To be honest, however, I share these thoughts with a bit of apprehension. I am not a pastor or a leader in this sense. I don't often find myself praying on behalf of a large group of people; I much more often am in contexts of community prayer, where many people are participating. Please take these thoughts as suggestions offered by one who is trying to help, not as accusations from one who is judging how you pray.

Many of the prayers recorded in Scripture are of the corporate prayer type. The Old Testament in particular records many of these prayers, such as Solomon's dedication of the temple (1 Kings 8:22ff.; 2 Chron 6:12ff.). Hezekiah's prayer in the face of threats from Sennacherib (2 Kings 19:14ff.; Is 37:14ff.) was probably also a time of corporate prayer. My suggestions regarding corporate prayer today do not draw from these scriptural prayers for a couple of reasons. First, the passages in which these prayers are recorded are narrative, not necessarily normative. While God answered both of these prayers, Scripture nowhere implies that we should be patterning our prayers after these. We are therefore free to learn from these prayers and decide for ourselves to what extent we should apply them.

Second, most of our corporate prayer today occurs in a context very different from those recorded in Scripture. The scriptural prayers mentioned above were prayed in contexts of times of special celebration or deep desperation. Most corporate prayer today happens in weekly worship services and takes the form of either an "opening" or "closing" prayer for the worship service. Some churches incorporate brief times of prayer in their actual worship times and a few may incorporate other corporate prayer times, but in general the opening and closing prayers are the most common. Of these two, the closing prayer tends to be the more significant in terms of the actual time devoted to it and the content it carries. Closing prayer itself tends to take one of two forms: either a relatively brief benediction or a more involved summary of the sermon topic.

Many speakers and pastors use a closing prayer time to address the congregation in one of a few different ways. First, the time is often used to summarize the sermon, restating one or more main points as a way of emphasizing them to the congregation. Second, the time is often used as a means of helping the congregation to apply the main lesson of the sermon. Finally, this time is sometimes used to exhort or encourage the congregation with regard to the theme of the sermon.

After all we've discussed regarding community prayer and the concept of addressing God rather than people in prayer, it will come as no surprise that I'd suggest this is not the best use of the closing prayer setting. This is not to say that the congregation doesn't need a summary or that they don't need an application or an encouragement. My suggestion is that these should be addressed directly to the congregation as a preparation for prayer rather than couched in terms of prayer themselves. The prayer time itself should be brief, direct and focused on asking God for his intervention. As we discussed in the previous chapter, such prayer not only focuses on God and honors him as the change agent in people's lives but also models for the congregation how they should pray on an ongoing basis regarding the issue around which the sermon was built.

Suppose the topic of the sermon has been forgiveness of others as a response to God's forgiveness. Most pastors would realize that there are people in their congregation who struggle with this and would probably feel a need to offer some sort of summary, restatement or encouragement at the end. It might sound something like this: "Father, many of us struggle in the area of forgiveness. But you have forgiven us so much that the wrongs done to us are relatively small. We need to remember your great mercy and love when we're tempted to hold grudges, and we need to pursue reconciliation with those who have offended us. We want to forgive others as you have forgiven us and so to bring you honor in all our relationships . . ."

Nothing untrue was said in the prayer above, but the fact that the entire prayer is all about the congregation and really addressed to the congregation makes it not really a prayer at all but rather a concluding exhortation to the congregation regarding an issue known to be a struggle. Likely, the congregation needs to be exhorted and even encouraged in this area; however, I suggest that prayer not only is not the place to do that, but is not an effective means for exhorting.

Consider the following alternative. The sermon ends and the pastor, rather than moving directly to closing prayer, addresses the congregation: "There are some of you here today who are struggling with this issue. You know that you should forgive someone who has wronged you, but you have not been able to actually do it. There may be any number of things making it difficult for you to forgive; but the God who forgave us for the death of his Son calls us to follow him in forgiveness. When you're struggling with this, go to that God in prayer and ask him to change your heart and give you a heart of forgiveness. We're going to do that now in prayer, and I encourage you to pray consistently about this if it's a struggle for you."

Then to God in prayer: "Father, please soften our hearts toward those who have wronged us. Give us your loving, forgiving grace toward others. Strengthen us and enable us to put aside offenses. Grow in us the character of Christ."

In this second scenario, rather than preaching to the congregation in prayer, the pastor has addressed the congregation directly, acknowledging the difficulty of forgiving while emphasizing the scriptural mandate. While the first prayer will likely have the effect of inducing guilt in those who are struggling with forgiveness, the second scenario presents a solution: take it to God in prayer. Rather than inducing guilt, this second scenario both acknowledges reality and offers hope for those struggling—the hope of leaning on God in prayer. The second prayer calls on God to change people's hearts, rather than making that the responsibility of the congregation. Finally, the second prayer models for the congregation a God-centered, effective response to the struggle with forgiveness; this becomes a pattern that the congregation can follow.

A simple, direct prayer like the second one is a prayer that is easily remembered and repeated by those in the congregation who most need to take this issue to God in prayer regularly. The first prayer does not empower them to deal with the issue in God's strength once they leave the service but rather pressures them to change. The second prayer empowers the congregation to actually become a more forgiving body by modeling for them the only thing they can really do about changing their hearts: pray. It is God who works in us to will and to act according to his good purpose, and as we encourage others to seek him in the midst of struggles, we offer the only real power for change. An unforgiving person simply cannot become a forgiving person without God's intervention. The first prayer implies that an unforgiving person can change in this way; but the second prayer acknowledges God as the only One who can bring about this change. As such, the first prayer doesn't offer real hope, but the second prayer does.

If you're a pastor reading this, have you ever despaired about the fact that you simply don't have enough time to pray for all the needs of your congregation? Do you realize that only God can make the changes needed in the hearts of your flock, but struggle with the fact that you can't adequately cover them in prayer? What if you could somehow empower the congregation to pray for themselves? What if you could model simple, direct, God-centered prayer that the congregation could follow in asking for God's intervention in their own lives? This is the possibility that the second scenario offers—a possibility that your congregation could learn how to invite God's work in their own lives in many different areas, with the result that God could answer those prayers and intervene in those situations.

One final way in which you might consider leading your congregation to grow in the area of seeking God for life-change is to actually encourage them to pray in small groups for each other and to provide time for that in the service. For example, in the scenario above, you might allow five minutes at the end for the congregation to actually pray for each other. You could instruct them to gather into groups of three or four; within each group, have one person introduce themself and give the name of someone they're having trouble forgiving. Have the group pray briefly over that and then move to the next person. Such a time needs to be led clearly, and it may take some people a few tries to understand and be able to participate fully; however, the power of having your congregation pray for each other is well worth the effort it takes.

PRAYER EVENTS
Prayer events are special times of corporate prayer often occasioned by some circumstance or celebration. Many churches, for example, plan events around the National Day of Prayer

or around the International Day of Prayer for the Persecuted Church. Sometimes different churches gather together for a citywide prayer event. The setting, circumstances and number of people can vary, but two common elements generally distinguish these events: they are gatherings specifically for the purpose of prayer, and they are composed of people who most likely do not pray regularly together.

In my experience, such gatherings are typically among the most problematic settings for effective prayer. This occurs for a number of reasons: lack of focus, inexperience in leading group prayer times, unfamiliarity with community prayer, differences in prayer theology and styles, to name a few.

Here's a common scenario. A "prayer event" is scheduled to last about an hour. The first half (or more) of that time is given to one or more speakers, who are nearly always speaking on topics not directly related to prayer. The gathering is then broken up into smaller groups (a good idea) to pray, but the people are given little or no instruction on how to pray together, other than the list of topics for which they will be praying. As you might guess, some of the groups may pray somewhat effectively together, but many will not.

Generally, a prerequisite for an effective prayer gathering is a focused topic. But it takes more than a compelling topic and a good speaker to make an effective prayer time. First and foremost, it takes leaders who themselves will bathe the gathering in prayer beforehand and who will set the environment and pace of the prayer meeting.

Let's pick a well-known type of prayer event and follow that through as an example. Many churches (or groups of churches) schedule special prayer events for the International Day of Prayer for the Persecuted Church (and many more probably should). Let's say you're planning an hourlong prayer event around this topic. Such prayer events will likely start off with a speaker speaking on some aspect of the persecuted church—whether a particular country where persecution is common, a plea for more concerted prayer and action on behalf of the persecuted church, or any other of a number of topics related to this subject. If you're organizing an event like this, you need to realize that most of the people who attend it already have some knowledge about the persecuted church and are already motivated to pray; that's why they are there. It's much more likely that they need instruction on how to pray effectively together than motivation to pray for the persecuted church.

As you consider how to set up the time, then, plan for some time of instruction regarding community prayer before actually breaking up for prayer. If you're planning to split the hour in half, for example (half for the speaker and half for prayer), consider giving the speaker fifteen minutes and then spending the next fifteen minutes in instruction on community prayer. Go beyond the typical cursory mentioning of good prayer practices and really teach for a few minutes on how to pray together effectively. Be sure to emphasize the importance of brevity and focus. Remove any performance pressure by making it okay for people to pray silently and encourage people to pray multiple times if God so leads them (but briefly each time).

If your gathering is a community gathering (that is to say, multiple churches are involved), then you need to say something about praying in tongues. Unless you know all the churches represented and are sure that no one there would pray in tongues, you need to address the issue explicitly. Set expectations clearly; it is generally recommended that in crosschurch prayer settings, praying in tongues not be practiced. If you know that one or more churches represented practices praying in tongues, you could (if you wish) request that the members of those churches pray together, so that all the people who are comfortable praying in tongues would be in the same groups. Don't underestimate the damaging effect that praying in tongues can have on unity in prayer when it is practiced among those who are unfamiliar or uncomfortable with it.

Generally, it's most effective in a prayer setting like this to break up the meeting into smaller prayer groups (of, say, five or six people) for the prayer time. Plan carefully how you will disseminate the information that you want to use for prayer; there are many ways to do this. You could have each group pray for a different country, using information and prayer requests you provide. It's important here not to give the groups too much to pray for, diminishing their focus. Encourage them to pray deeply about one subject rather than to skim over many subjects.

Finally, as is the case with small group prayer, realize that not all prayer events look alike. I've never been to a South Korean prayer meeting, for example, but from what I understand, the practice there is for everyone to pray at the same time, creating what some have described as a wall of sound. This, of course, precludes the type of praying in agreement that comes from hearing what someone else is praying and adding on to it, but there is no doubt that these congregations are nonetheless praying in unity and praying very effectively. Effective corporate prayer does not look exactly the same everywhere it's practiced. Still, the principles in this chapter should help you think about how to make your prayer event as effective as it can be.

Corporate prayer settings—whether a congregational worship meeting or an interchurch prayer event—can be great ways to promote unity and growth in prayer. When well led, these settings can inspire and empower the personal prayer lives of those who participate, as well as being sweet times of community in God's presence. Prayerful planning, preparation and leading of these times will pay significant dividends in the effectiveness of the prayer.

If you lead times of corporate prayer, be intentional about how you set up the time and how you lead it. Pay attention to details like the logistics of breaking a large group up into small groups for prayer. Communicate very clearly the expectations of how the group will pray together. Emphasis on particulars like these will help ensure a prayer time that is orderly, God-focused and effective in the minds of all the participants.

QUESTIONS FOR DISCUSSION/REFLECTION

1. How would you characterize your personal prayer times? Are you focused and attentive or does your mind tend to wander? How could the principles in this chapter improve your prayer times?

2. Think of situations in which you have prayed one-on-one

with someone. How (if at all) will you pray differently the next time?

3. Picture yourself leading an interchurch prayer meeting. What would you emphasize in order to help the group pray together most effectively?

CONCLUSION

TOGETHER IN PRAYER

IT IS OFTEN SAID THAT PRAYER IS an expression of relationship with God. Community prayer, then, is an expression of a community's relationship with God, or, from an individual's standpoint, it's a relationship with God and others. Although all relationships differ as all people differ, there are some common guidelines for developing and maintaining good relationships. It should not be surprising then, that there are some common guidelines for community prayer.

As we've seen throughout this book, these guidelines follow from the overall context of praying to God with people. Praying to God (as opposed to praying to people) means that we're addressing God in prayer; that the requests we're making are being made of him, not of others in the group; and that our prayers are focused on him, not on circumstances. Praying with people means that we're keeping our prayers brief and focused, and that we're listening to each other and agreeing with one another.

Since prayer is in its essence relationship, the application of these guidelines will vary from group to group. That's why there are no definite answers to questions like, "How long is too long to pray?" Answers to questions like this vary, depending on the relationships and experience of group members, but a good general answer is, "Shorter than most people think"!

No one prayer, prayer model or prayer format can possibly reflect all of what Scripture intends prayer to be—not the prayer of Jabez, not the apostolic prayers, not John 17, not even the Lord's Prayer. The A.C.T.S. format is a great teaching tool but is not all of what prayer is meant to be. Prayer will always be more than we think it is, because God is bigger than we can possibly imagine.

As a result, it is not the purpose of this book to propose a "one size fits all" set of specific rules to govern community prayer times. Rather, our goal has been to explore principles for community prayer and to try to derive some helpful practices from those principles. Generally, these practices will help any small group to pray more meaningfully together and to experience more completely the relationship with God and with each other that community prayer should represent.

We began by noting that there are some fundamental differences between community prayer and private prayer, and by postulating that we could derive some principles for community prayer from Scripture. We applied principles of humility, love and orderliness to community prayer. We developed some practices based on those principles. We offered some suggestions of how to lead the prayer time and tried to apply those suggestions in settings of different kinds of groups. We touched on different prayer styles and emphases, and wrapped up by looking at how community prayer principles might apply in other prayer settings.

You may have gotten to this point and wondered, "So, what next? How do I actually implement some of these principles and practices?" In this chapter, I will offer some suggestions for next steps, as well as some hope and inspiration for you as you embark on a new adventure in community prayer.

The focus of this book has been on prayer in a small group setting. I have chosen this particular focus because I believe that small group prayer in most churches has the best chance for actually releasing the power of God through the church and because I think it's a neglected area both of practice and of teaching. Although most churches probably have individuals who pray well—that is, whose practice of prayer is consistent, God-centered and effective—most of those same churches don't pray as well as they could as churches. I believe the best place to address this is in small groups.

The principles in this book are not limited to church small groups, however. Hopefully, if you're involved in a campus small group or a neighborhood group you have seen some value in practicing community prayer more intentionally. I first learned to pray in a small group setting in my Inter-Varsity chapter in college, and most of my richest and most memorable community prayer experiences still date from those days.

It would be a mistake to assume that your entire group

has the same level of interest and vision that you do. Chances are, in order to significantly improve your group's experience of community prayer, you're going to need to bring the group along by stages. Your efforts must be marked by much prayer and patience on your part. The suggestions I'm going to make in this chapter assume that you have the influence in your group to carry them out—either because you're the small group leader or because you have secured permission from your small group leader to take charge of the prayer time and to grow the group in prayer. If neither of these is true, then of course you'll need to engage your small group leader before attempting to apply these principles in your group.

If your group is not praying together regularly, then the place to start is to cast a vision for prayer in your small group. Use the Scriptures. And, of course, pray that God will raise up a commitment to community prayer in the group and that he will grant you favor in the eyes of group members as you grow together in this area.

If your group does pray together regularly, but doesn't pray *well* together, then you need to prayerfully examine the reasons for that. Probably one or more of the principles of community prayer is being unintentionally violated. You'll have to tailor your teaching and encouragement to the group. Begin by asking yourself some questions to help you get at the bottom of what's wrong with your group's prayer time. Is it largely focused on sharing and very little on prayer? Do one or two people dominate the time while most remain silent? Are your prayers focused on circumstances? Are all the requests that your group brings for prayer surface issues, and are the deeper issues of spiritual growth being neglected? Do your group members tend to preach to each other as they pray? The answers to these and other questions that you bring to God in prayer will determine what you need to emphasize in order to grow your group's community prayer life.

If your group is like most small groups, then whatever prayer time you do have together likely tends to focus on requests that the group members bring. This is actually a great focus to have, as the small group should be the primary place (outside the family, perhaps) where people give and receive prayer. Usually, the place where things get off track, and therefore the first place to look for ways to improve the focus, is in the time of sharing prayer requests. Help your group keep in mind a couple of things:

- The whole point of the sharing time is simply to gather information to help you pray. It's not a "catch-up" time.

- The time of sharing, not the prayer time, is where the explanations should take place.

- Try to get your group to move over time to sharing and praying about deeper spiritual issues rather than focusing solely on temporal situations. Even when praying about temporary situations, focus on kingdom prayers (this will take some time).

In most groups, the expectations of the prayer time are not communicated clearly, leaving each person to interpret for themselves what might be good practices. Realistically, most people are not very intentional about how they pray in a group setting, so the group prayer time can often become disjointed. You can alleviate this problem by explaining the reasons behind how you're leading the prayer time to the group members. Take the time to explain to them the principles of community prayer. Don't expect them to understand or practice all of them right away; normally, people will require some time to adjust their prayer habits and styles to fit into an effective community prayer setting. You might try incorporating one principle or practice at a time to help the group adjust. (If you're going to go this route, I strongly recommend starting with the practice of praying briefly.)

As your group begins to grow together in prayer, some of your group members will catch on more quickly than others. Be patient and prayerful about this. If you feel that someone needs extra instruction or even correction, be sure to address the person alone, not in front of the group. Watch out that your group does not develop a critical spirit regarding prayer—a sense of superiority on the part of some and judgmentalism toward those who aren't "getting it." Watch out also for the types of prayer that can be divisive. The whole point of community prayer is that it is a community relationship with God. Disunity within the group by definition destroys what community prayer is attempting to accomplish.

Be open to different prayer styles within your group. Some people pray very matter-of-factly; others pray more emotionally. Some people are more "mystical" in the way they pray than others. Some people are list-oriented, while others would see that as very limiting. Within the principles and practices of good community prayer, there is room for different styles and emphases. Generally, if your group members are praying briefly, focused on God and agreeing together in prayer, then your community prayer life is on track, regardless of the different prayer styles practiced.

As time goes on and your group begins to regularly practice the principles of community prayer, you'll want to challenge your group to grow in other prayer areas, such as confession and praise. Intercession for others outside your group can be a good "mission" for your group. Be creative in introducing some prayer exercises to the group to keep the group growing and stretching. Pay attention to any "prayer passions" in your group, and encourage group members to explore and develop passions in prayer.

Encourage your group to express how they feel about where the group is heading in prayer. Look for feedback and incorporate ideas as you can. The more attention you pay to the group's prayer life, the more your group members will get the idea that prayer is not incidental to their time together but is really fundamental to group life.

I hope that you finish this book not only with some ideas for how to improve your group's community prayer life but also with hope and vision for what that prayer life could be. I firmly believe, based on experience, that the principles and practices we've discussed will make a difference in your group's prayer life. In reality, however, only the working of the Holy Spirit in your group and in each group member will truly revolutionize your prayer time together. It is the Holy Spirit who teaches us how to pray, and who intercedes for us with groanings that we cannot even imagine. It is he who understands our hearts, who can cleanse what needs cleansing, strengthen what needs strengthening, and knit together our hearts and minds in true community prayer.

Therefore, I hope you finish this book in an attitude of prayer, for that is the attitude in which it was written. All the teaching, all the exercises, all the experience in the world cannot replace simple, humble reliance on God's intervention. At the bottom, it is he who will transform your group's prayer life into what he wants it to be. Don't worry if you're "getting through" to group members; pray that God will be the one who gets through. That's what I'm praying for you.

QUESTIONS FOR DISCUSSION/REFLECTION

1. What did you find to be stretching or challenging in this book?

2. Think back over small groups of which you've been a member. Was there anything in this book that could have helped them pray better?

3. If you're in a small group right now, how effectively does that group pray together? Which principles or practices you read in this book or thought of while you read could help the group pray more effectively?

APPENDIX A

YOUR GROUP'S PRAYER QUOTIENT

How "prayer-friendly" is your small group? Take a couple of moments, either individually or as a group, to think through the following questions and score your group as indicated. See below for scoring assessment.

_____ 1. How often does your small group pray together?

    0 = Never

    1 = Rarely, or only when there is a special need

    2 = About half the time

    3 = Usually

_____ 2. When your group prays together, how much time do you tend to spend praying?

    0 = We don't pray together.

    1 = Very little; typically only one person prays

    2 = Some

    3 = A significant amount

_____ 3. What kinds of things does your group pray about?

    0 = We don't pray together.

    1 = Just an opening/closing prayer or prayer for a special need in a member's life

    2 = We regularly pray for each other's concerns.

    3 = We pray for each other and for people/ concerns outside the group.

____ 4. How many people typically participate when you pray together?

  0 = We don't pray together.

  1 = Usually just one

  2 = A few

  3 = The majority of the group

____ 5. Which of the following comes closest to how you'd describe your group prayer time?

  0 = We don't pray.

  1 = It usually drags or is too short to have a pace.

  2 = It varies.

  3 = It seems lively and fast-paced.

____ 6. How would you rate the sense of unity in your group's prayer?

  0 = We don't pray together.

  1 = People tend to pray according to their own agendas and priorities.

  2 = It varies.

  3 = We regularly experience significant unity and agreement.

____ 7. After prayer, is there typically a sense among the group of having been in God's presence?

  0 = We don't pray together.

  1 = Rarely

  2 = Sometimes

  3 = Usually

____ **Total Score**

Assessment

All groups are different, but hopefully these generalizations will help you understand how your group is doing in prayer.

Score: 0-10: Your group is having significant difficulty praying together. Consider reviewing chapter six as a group and trying to develop a common understanding of community prayer.

Score: 11-16: Your group is doing fairly well, but there is room for improvement. See below for suggestions about specific areas to target related to each question.

Score: 17-21: Your group is praying well together. Consider stretching your group's prayer muscles with suggestions from chapters eight and nine, if appropriate.

If you would like to see your group improve in a specific area, consider the suggestions below:

Question 1. If your group does not pray together often, review chapter six together, or perhaps have the group read the entire book together. Remember, you will need to cast a vision; some in your group may be ready for a community prayer life while others are not.

Question 2. Consider how you are currently allocating your group time. If prayer tends to be the last thing you do, consider moving it earlier in your time together. You may also want to consider devoting a meeting every so often specifically to prayer.

Question 3. Chapter nine has suggestions for praying "beyond the walls" of your small group. Also, if your prayers for each other tend to avoid deeper, spiritual issues, consider incorporating confession. You may first need to lay some groundwork in order to build an appropriate level of trust. If you don't pray regularly for each other, review chapter seven for suggestions on how to do this effectively.

Question 4. If your prayer time is dominated by a handful of people and there are some who do not regularly participate, try to understand the reasons behind the lack of participation. If people are feeling intimidated, it could be because some in the group are praying too long or are preaching to the group in their prayers. Consider breaking the group into partners for prayer time, putting people together who do not participate regularly to protect them from being dominated by the more outgoing pray-ers.

Question 5. If you sense that a significant amount of your prayer time is being devoted to information sharing, find a way to move that outside the prayer time. If your prayer time tends to drag, people are probably praying too long. Consider praying for one person (or topic) at a time to break up a prayer time that seems to drag. Long periods of silence can (though does not necessarily) indicate that the group is not praying in unity and lacks direction. Review chapter five with your group to help the group build an understanding of agreement in prayer.

Question 6. If there is not a sense of unity in your group, review chapter five to see if this could be rooted in the way that people are praying. If there is a lot of skipping around in prayer, give some instruction on listening to one another. If the group tends to pray agenda-based prayers, review chapter four for help on focusing prayer on God's will and his kingdom.

Question 7. If the group does not have a sense of having been in God's presence, the most likely cause is that prayers are horizontally focused. Review chapters three and four. Analyze whether prayers are being directed toward God or toward people. Consider devoting some time specifically to praise and thanksgiving. Reviewing Scriptures that focus on God's character may help with this.

APPENDIX B

BIBLIOGRAPHY & RECOMMENDED RESOURCES

BIBLIOGRAPHY

Brother Lawrence. *The Practice of the Presence of God.* Peabody, Mass.: Hendrickson, 2004.

Foster, Richard J. *Celebration of Discipline: The Path to Spiritual Growth.* New York: HarperCollins, 1998.

———. *Prayer: Finding the Heart's True Home.* New York: HarperCollins, 1992.

Frazee, Randy. *Making Room for Life.* Grand Rapids: Zondervan, 2003.

Peretti, Frank. *Piercing the Darkness.* Westchester, Ill.: Crossway, 1989.

RECOMMENDED PUBLICATIONS

Hunter, W. Bingham. *The God Who Hears.* Downers Grove, Ill.: InterVarsity Press, 1986.

Johnstone, Patrick. *Operation World,* 21st Century ed. Johnson City, Tenn.: STL Distribution, 2005.

Jones, Timothy. *The Art of Prayer.* New York: Doubleday, 2005.

Pray! Magazine. Colorado Springs: NavPress. <www.pray mag.com>

ONLINE RESOURCES

Church Prayer Leaders Network <www.prayerleader.com>. Resources for leaders of church prayer ministries.

Global Prayer Digest <www.global-prayer-digest.org>. Daily prayer guide for unreached people groups around the world, including an optional email subscription.

International Christian Concern <www.persecution.org>. Prayer guides and other materials related to the persecuted church around the world.

National Day of Prayer. <www.nationaldayofprayer.org>. A resource designed to encourage participation in the annual National Day of Prayer, and to pray effectively throughout the year.

Operation World <www.operationworld.org>. A global reference for church and mission groups.

The Presidential Prayer Team <www.presidentialprayerteam. org>. Weekly prayer requests for national leaders, including an optional email subscription.